"Barb Newman was an in: whose vision for inclu: Christian congregations many insights from Barb's  into this volume by Victoria White. May many more congregations and ministries be transformed by the Holy Spirit as they read this material and discern pathways for more fruitful ministry with everyone."

- **John D. Witvliet**
Director, Calvin Institute of Christian Worship.

"If we Christians from evangelical and reformed traditions had saints, Barb Newman would surely be among their number. Worship as One is a capstone to her incredible ministry career as the seminal authority on disability inclusion in Christian schools and inclusive worship in the American church. Pastors and other church leaders will discover a lifetime of practical wisdom and experience in disability ministry in this book."

- **Stephen Grcevich**
MD, President and Founder, Key Ministry.
Author of *Mental Health and the Church: A Ministry Handbook for Including Children and Adults with ADHD, Anxiety, Mood Disorders, and Other Common Mental Health Conditions.*

"Among the many voices speaking into the field of disability ministry, Barb Newman's is one of the clearest. Her decades of work helping churches has informed this important book that serves as a fitting legacy to her exceptional career. Packed with illustrations and examples, Barb offers a strong 3-part plan that includes wisdom from special education situated within a strong biblical framework. Barb's writing style makes it easy for those newer to disability-related discussions to enter deeply into these critical conversations. Additionally, those of us who have been at this work for a while will also find fresh insights and practical strategies to help God's people truly worship as one."

- **Thomas Boehm**
Ph.D., M.Div, Director of Wheaton Center for Faith and Disability Ann Haskins Associate Professor of Special Education Coordinator of Special Education Program, Wheaton College.

"Barbara Newman has been one of the most profound and prophetic voices in the movement to help churches become more disability inclusive. This book leaves no stone unturned as she leads the church into the future of doing ministry with those who identify as disabled. Barbara's words of wisdom are simultaneously both a gift and a vision for what the church must look like if it is to model God's vision for oneness and inclusion. This book is essential reading for those who have a passion for imitating the mission, mindset, and ministry of Jesus."

- **Lamar Hardwick D.Min**
Lead Pastor, Tri- Cities Church.

"No one is better suited to help churches become places of belonging for people with disabilities than Barb Newman. That's why this short manual for churches, collected and edited posthumously, is so vital for pastors and church ministry leaders. Here's why: You as a pastor or leader are tempted to presume that there are too many things you don't know about disabilities. But Barb reminds you that all you are called to do is to respond to the ones who come to your church doors, who make your church family complete, who make it possible for your church to be a "complete *body." More than that, though, Barb makes the complicated and complex manageable. So, please use and share this book within your church leadership team. Study it together. And while you're at it, make sure to look up Barb's video on puzzle pieces. That alone will give you the context to understand the full value of this book in helping to complete your church family."*

- **Dan VanderPlaats**
Vice President of Advancement, Marketing and Communications
Elim Christian Services.

"Barb Newman's final words to us are bitter sweet. The sadness is that they are her last spoken words to us but the sweetness is that with her usual style of grace and generosity she shared the wisdom that God worked through her throughout her life and her ministry. Barb told us that it doesn't take fancy tricks or strategies to make people welcome. It just takes generosity and hospitality to make people feel welcome and valued as they are, as we all are as children of God. Barb does have great strategies but what makes them so powerful is their simplicity and the way she shares them with all of us. Thank you Barb, you are missed."

- **Anne M. Masters**
Ph.D., FAAIDD, Director, Archdiocese of Newark Office for Pastoral Ministry with Persons with Disabilities.

Worship

as

ONE

Varied Abilities in the Body of Christ

By Barbara J. Newman

Edited by Victoria White

Copyright ©2022 All Belong

All Rights Reserved

Barbara J. Newman is the author of the original manuscript for this book. However, she was unable to complete edits to the manuscript for publication before she went home to Jesus. With generous support from donors and the hard work of staff, All Belong presents this book in its final form, edited by Victoria White, as one way to carry on her legacy.

Examples and stories used in this book may have names or other information altered to protect confidentiality.

Unless otherwise noted, all Scripture references in this book are taken from The Holy Bible, New International Version®, NIV®. Copyright © 1973, 1978, 1984, 2011 by Biblica, Inc.® Used by permission of Zondervan. All rights reserved worldwide. www.Zondervan.com. The "NIV" and "New International Version" are trademarks registered in the United States Patent and Trademark Office by Biblica, Inc. ®

Dedication

Barbara Newman wished to dedicate this book with love to four women who were life-long encouragers in times of celebration and accomplishment, dependable anchors during difficult seasons, and daily reminders that family is one of God's absolute best gifts in life.

To my treasured sisters:

Nancy Lou Stob

Ruth Ann Bandstra (in memorium)

Sue Marie Hamstra

Mary Beth Ippel

Acknowledgements

This congregational resource book is not the work of one individual. I thank God for the people and organizations who have made contributions to this work and to my life.

Barry Newman, you are my dear husband who brainstorms with me, encourages me, anchors me, tells me when to stop working, and is my best friend. James, John, and Jasmine Newman, you are my treasured children who have taught me so much about community and being there for one another. I love each of you so very much.

Victoria White, thank you not only for fleshing out the section on wrap-around support teams, but you have spent many hours helping me locate the right word, paragraph indent, and thought picture for this work. As always, you are my professional complement and strong friend.

Dr. Thomas B. Hoeksema Sr. and Dr. John D. Witvliet, your words to all of us about perspective through Scripture are inviting, compelling, and life changing. Thank you for the gift of these words and for the many other words you have both spoken into my life – words that have molded and shaped my career and writing.

Dr. Maria Cornou and Rev. Dr. LaTonya Penny, you have done ground-breaking research in thinking about congregational response and individuals with disabilities within a variety of cultural settings. Thank you for work and what it has taught me.

All Belong Center for Inclusive Education (formerly CLC Network), I am so thankful for my colleagues and the way you have supported, encouraged, directed, and influenced me as well as the information in this book. I praise God for the powerful impact you have in communities across North America. Special thanks to Katie and Elizabeth for your support in so many ways on this book journey.

Calvin Institute of Christian Worship (CICW), it has been my delight to learn from you and with you in the area of worship. It's an honor to be a partner affiliate and I am energized by the passionate, knowledgeable staff and well-planned events.

Zeeland Christian School, every school day you paint a picture of I Corinthians 12 –one body together in Christ –that is breathtaking and yet as natural as breathing. I am honored to be a part of this God-honoring portrait.

Congregations featured in this book, your fine leadership and strong vision for communities where people of all abilities belong is a gift to those of us wanting to learn from you. I have enjoyed time in each of your congregations. Thank you for leading the way.

-Barbara J. Newman

This publication was made possible by a donor who believes that community is incomplete without each puzzle piece, sharing our passion for transforming Christian communities into places of belonging for people of all abilities.

Contributions to this work have continued beyond Barbara's writing. Thanks to the editorial support of Dirk Buursma, insights on community teams from Joy Anderson, contributions to the visual beauty by Mariah Scott with input from Samantha Gossard Dykstra, improvements suggested by the "peanut gallery" (White family), encouragement of colleagues, collaborators, and congregations who have looked forward to this book, and the continued blessing and support of the Newman family. She won't be forgotten, Barry.

Table of Contents

Introduction i

Part 1 Perspective: Puzzle Pieces 1
1: Introduction to Perspective: Puzzle Pieces 3
2: Scriptural Perspective 11
3: Puzzle Piece Learning from Congregations 19
4: Puzzle Piece Take-Aways 23
5: Reflections by Dr. Thomas Hoeksema and Dr. John Witvliet 27
6: Practical Tools for Your Congregation 41

Part 2 Participation: Universal Design 45
7: Introduction to Participation: Universal Design 47
8: Learning from Congregations Using Universal Design 57
9: Practical Tools for Your Congregation: 61

Part 3 Personalization: Responsive Design 73
10: Introduction to Personalization: Responsive Design 75
11: Responsive Design Process 79
12: Cultural Considerations for Personalized Plans 89
13: Becoming Community Using Teams by Victoria White 93
14: Learning from Congregations using Responsive Design 109
15: Practical Tools for Your Congregation: 115

Part 4: The 3-Part Plan in Action 127
16: The 3-Part Plan In Infant & Toddler Ministry 129
17: The 3-Part Plan In Children & Youth Ministry 141
18: The 3-Part Plan In Worship Settings 163

Closing: Two Experiences with a Reminder to Put God at the Center 194
References 200

Introduction

Many congregations put up welcome signs, set out welcome mats, and hold day-long conferences on how to be welcoming. It's important for visitors and members alike to know that there is a place of welcome and belonging within that community of believers. Just as God throws out the welcome red carpet into His kingdom, we seek to mirror God's heart as we welcome adults and children into our congregations.

A welcome, however, is not a one-sided act. The words and practices that spring up around the word *welcome* are then received by an individual. To be most effective, that person must interpret those actions as welcoming. For example, a person shaking your hand may have the best intention of being welcoming, but if that grip is too tight on your hand with arthritis, or if you happen to see the person coughing into his hand before shaking your own, you may not interpret this gesture as hospitable as it was intended to be.

Imagine...

A pastor's invitation to partake of the Lord's Supper to all those who believe in Jesus as Lord and Savior. What sounds like a word of welcome to participate may actually be the sound of a door slamming shut if one of the believers is searching for the nonexistent gluten-free bread or wafer option.

A youth leader's invitation to a community treasure hunt event for "all youth, grades six to twelve." While it may sound like everyone is welcome, when the eleventh grader who is a wheelchair user shows up for the event, it's clear the event is closed to that individual. No one had thought through the accessibility issues that would have truly allowed each member of that age group to participate.

The church initiative introducing adult small groups in several locations for the fall book study. The sign-up sheet forgot to mention that in order to participate, people would need to be proficient readers, writers, and speakers who are able to access evening transportation.

What congregations intend to be a welcoming practice can be the opposite for several individuals. How can they make some changes so that more people can receive a welcome and find a place of belonging instead of rejection or exclusion?

Three Parts Create a Holistic Plan

In this book, I will define a three-part plan that will equip a church community to better include persons with varied abilities in worship, youth and adult education programs, and other events. The plan is simple:

1. Perspective: Puzzle Pieces
2. Participation: Universal Design
3. Personalization: Responsive Design

In the first three sections of the book, I define key features of each part of the plan and highlight some examples from congregations. There will be activities you can use in your congregation to learn more and apply that portion of the three-part plan. The last section of this book will feature practical application of the plan in these areas: infant/toddler areas, children and youth ministries, and corporate worship settings. Samples and links to templates and other resources are included in the "Practical Tools." These will equip you for inclusive ministry in your own congregation.

The leadership of the church must be on board with this plan for it to work. That is so important, I might have put it as the first part, making this a 4-part plan!

- The leadership's perspective is where this plan will have a firm foundation or be washed away.
- The leadership's pursuit of participation through universal design will make the changes happen that are necessary.
- The leadership's support of personalization through responsive design is what will ensure it is done and done well.

The plan for your congregation requires leadership be on board.

Leadership that is on board will see value in having a person or committee to coordinate and oversee it working in the church. Many denominations and local churches have roles such as Accessibility Coordinator, Pastor of Care, Disability Ministry Director, Disability Advocate – someone who would get the phone call when a new family wants to come but needs to know what the church will do to welcome their family member with a disability. In the chapters on Responsive Design are further details about this role, but here I want to mention that such a role is a great one to be cheering the leadership on and holding the church accountable to keeping the plan going. If the church is a casserole, I think of this person or committee as the shredded cheese throughout the whole thing, supporting and adding the right flavor to all the other ingredients.

It is my hope and prayer that after learning about the three-part plan and a variety of practical applications, congregations will extend welcome through greeters, the Lord's Supper, youth group, adult small groups, and other programs and events—all of which will lead to places of belonging within our churches for people of all abilities.

A Note on How to Use This Book

The content in this book is both the "why" and the "how" of inclusive ministry. You may wish to read the "why" portions in each part before you get into the "how" aspects. For that reason, each section contains ideas and explanations (the "why") followed by chapters titled "Learning from Congregations" and "Practical Tools" (the "how")

Part 1
Perspective: Puzzle Pieces

Defining Puzzle Piece Perspective

Puzzle Piece Perspective is a visual way of thinking about God's design for individuals as well as communities.

1

Introduction to Perspective: Puzzle Pieces

What do you see? As you look at the picture on this page, can you tell what it is?

Right now, your brain is working overtime to classify and identify pieces of that picture as it attempts to make meaning of that visual message. It may help to tell you that the photographer was standing awfully close to that object before snapping the photo. Make a guess. The actual full photo is on the next page.

In some respects, the word *disability* can also bring up a picture in someone's mind. Your brain will make meaning of that word based on your experiences. Perhaps you are picturing a person in your life who has some sort of disability. Perhaps you are thinking of a parking spot designated for someone whose license plate on their vehicle has a matching symbol. Perhaps you are recalling a book you read that highlighted a particular area of disability.

It's important to make sure we can all see the full picture of the puzzle rather than one small piece. Since each of us comes with our limited view and experience with disability in ministry, to begin this conversation let's look at some myths that surface in many congregations, as well as define some important images from Scripture through a True-False quiz. Complete the quiz before you read on to find the answers.

True or False:

1. About 10 percent of persons in the United States have some sort of a disability. True or False?

2. There is a family who tried taking their 3-year-old son with autism to Sunday school and were told never to bring him back again because they "could not handle him here". The family then took turns attending church for the next 4 years while one of the parents stayed at home with their son. True or False?

3. The best way to support people with disabilities in church is to build a separate program and hire experts to run that program. True or False?

4. The reason churches most often give, in Barbara Newman's experience, for excluding a person with a disability is that they do not see a clear Scriptural reason for including that person. True or False?

5. The ideas in this book are only helpful for people with identified disabilities. True or False?

6. In all likelihood, I too will need this type of understanding or support in my congregation at some stage in my life. True or False?

7. I am not trained in any of these areas and therefore do not have a role in making this type of initiative successful in my congregation. True or False?

Here are the answers along with information to understand the truth behind each statement.

1. *About 10 percent of persons in the United States have some sort of a disability.* **False**. While statistics vary between states and countries, the United States Census looks at this statistic every ten years. According to census results, disability impacts nearly 20 percent of the population. The Center for Disease Control states that more than 25 percent of adults have some sort of disability.[1] This was determined using a set of six questions, found on the CDC website.[2] That is at least one in every five people, if not one in every four!

2. *A family that tried to bring their three-year-old son with autism to Sunday school was told never to bring him back again because "we cannot handle him here." The family took turns attending church for the next four years while one of the parents stayed at home with their son.* **True**. While it's hard to imagine someone at church telling parents never to bring their child back again, this is a very common story. This story is told to and about both children and adults with disabilities.

3. *The best way to support people with disabilities in church is to build a separate program and hire experts to run that program.* **False**. While that may seem logical at first, we will consider alternate and more effective ways to envision supports and options for people of varied abilities.

---

[1] See "Disability and Health Overview," Centers for Disease Control and Prevention, September 16, 2020, www.cdc.gov/ncbddd/disabilityandhealth/disability.html.
[2] See "Disability Datasets," Centers for Disease Control and Prevention, September 16, 2020, cdc.gov/ncbddd/disabilityandhealth/datasets.html.

4. *The reason churches most often give, in Barbara Newman's experience, for excluding a person with a disability is that they do not see a clear Scriptural reason for including that person.* **False.** Despite that compelling call from Scripture and congregations being certain of the "why" they should include the reason most congregations have given me is that they don't know the "how."

5. *The ideas in this book are only helpful for people with identified disabilities.* **False.** How many people comment that one of the most memorable parts of the worship service was the children's message? An overwhelming number of people suggest they remember best through pictures and visuals in comparison with very few people who remember best with a "words only" approach.

6. *In all likelihood, I too will need this type of understanding or support in my congregation at some stage in my life.* **True.** Think back to that category of individuals who have a diagnosed area of disability. Whether it's due to the aging process or it's a stage of time due to illness or injury, we all benefit very personally from getting better at this three-part plan.

7. *I am not trained in any of these areas and therefore do not have a role in making this type of initiative successful in my congregation.* **False.** While some guidance might be helpful along the way, we have found that any person with any role in the church needs to be knowledgeable about this three-part plan.

Important thoughts to ponder with these truths:

Who is included in the 20 to 25 percent of the population with disabilities? If we take a trip through an average church, starting in the church nursery and moving through to the group made up of senior citizens, we may encounter people with disabilities in every area. We may see an infant born with spina bifida, a toddler with Down syndrome, an elementary-aged child with a learning disability or attention-deficit/hyperactivity disorder (ADHD), a youth with autism spectrum disorder, an adult with Bi-polar Disorder, and an aging adult with limited vision, memory, hearing, or mobility. It's a huge group of people! It is evident that official numbers do not even fully capture the true percentage of people with disabilities in our communities.

In our tour of the average church, we may also notice how churches have become quite good at building programs. There are children's ministries, youth ministries, women's and men's ministries, seniors' ministries, worship ministries, evangelism and outreach ministries, and a number of others. I often equate these programs to the canned goods that make up a large congregational casserole. Congregations seem to think in "cans." Therefore, it's a natural step to say, "Let's set up a disability ministry can." Some congregations even secure a space and open "Room 9" for the "special needs ministry." If you already have a separate program or even a "Room 9," please continue to read. As you will soon find out, this book is not only about that 20 percent of the population identified with some sort of disability; it's about 100 percent of your community and our ability to better function as one body together in Christ that more closely resembles the "shredded cheese" that binds the whole casserole together as opposed to another "can" added to the recipe.

In more than thirty years of working with congregations, I cannot recall even one church that has given some sort of biblical reason why Amy should not participate in worship or Carlos should not be allowed in youth group. In fact, most can cite many Bible passages that encourage them to include every person. What many ministry leaders did say, however, is, "We don't know how to include persons with varied abilities in worship or education, in fellowship or service opportunities."

Here is the great news: the pages in this book and linked resources are overflowing with the "how to." And the strategies, ideas, and best practices in this book are for everyone! The very purpose of part 2 ("Participation: Universal Design") is to show that the ideas create better options for 100 percent of the community. If you're not convinced at this point, check back in after reading through part 2.

As for who needs to know this, let's ask a few more questions: Do you purchase products for the restrooms at your church? Do you ever speak through a microphone? Do you have any role as a volunteer in the educational programs? Are you a greeter, cookie baker, or bulletin designer? Then you are part of making this plan come to life in your community.

2

Scriptural Perspective

Tucked away somewhere in my car, luggage, desk, or dresser drawer, I am never far away from one of my favorite visuals—a puzzle piece that is colored half pink and half green. This example not only highlights God's creative work in each one of us, but it also references God's design for the communities we form.

Psalm 139:13-14 talks about God as a master creator, interacting individually with each one of us in that creative process.

"For you created my inmost being; you knit me together in my mother's womb.

I praise you because I am fearfully and wonderfully made; your works are wonderful, I know that full well."

If we consider the hands of God with a pair of knitting needles and a knitting pattern that is unique to each one of us, I often picture the colors of the yarn as green and pink. The green stitches represent the areas of strength and gifting present in each of us. The pink stitches represent the areas of challenge and struggle. As we look at this totally unique, God-designed knitting project, we begin to see that the green and pink puzzle piece can actually represent each of us. We are all a combination of gifts and challenges, strengths, and struggles. I am that puzzle piece, and so are you.

In fact, I could introduce myself to you by way of my puzzle piece. As an author and speaker, you can imagine that "words" are part of my green. I love words. I enjoy reading and writing words. Speaking words is also quite fun for me. Sign me up for a great game of Scrabble, Boggle, Quiddler, or Words with Friends. In fact, playing word games with my online friends is a fantastic way to end a perfect day filled with words!

Pink for me, however, would be anything that involves hand-eye coordination. This became evident to my children at young ages. They would invite me to play those games with controllers and come out the winners every time. Looking even further back, I was the fourth grader standing up against the playground fence every time at recess, chosen last for the team to play any sort of sport involving hitting, kicking, hurling, blocking, or whiffing any sort of ball. While I enjoy watching a great game of football, yelling out encouraging WORDS to the players on the field, my spot on the sidelines is well suited for my puzzle piece!

What about you? If you were to notice something green about your own God-designed puzzle piece, what would that area of strength or gifting be? What is a pink area for you? Just to get the self-discovery juices flowing, most of us would consider some of the following areas as either green or pink: paying attention, solving visual puzzles, remembering best the things we see (or the things we hear), drawing, sports, technology, or social skills.

The list could be quite long and certainly could include some of the gifts of the Spirit described in Scripture (Isaiah 11:2–3; Romans 12:3–8; 1 Corinthians 12:8–10, Ephesians 4:7–13). Consider some of your greens and pinks in administration, teaching, prophecy, or hospitality. Using the puzzle piece here, pick out two or three of your green gifts and one or two of your pink struggles. It may be an idea I mentioned here, or it could be a skill or deficit you have in baking, auto mechanics, or board gaming. There is a spot for your name in the middle of the puzzle piece and notice the tag on the edge, which reads, "Handmade by God"—a truth stamped on each of our lives.

Puzzle Pieces and Persons with Disabilities

While it's interesting to consider the application of puzzle pieces to each of our lives, I have noticed some patterns about puzzle pieces as it relates to persons with disabilities. Sometimes a person with a disability is considered an "all pink" person. Instead of noticing the greens stitched by God into that person, the disability seems to be the most noticeable feature of that individual – and people see pink.

- Down syndrome Jonathan
- Autistic Sue
- Wheelchair Carlos
- Bi-Polar Mykaela
- Dementia Annabelle
- Slow Reader Tyrone

When people see an "all pink" person, it's easy to respond with pity or react only as a caregiver. In his book *Including People with Disabilities in Faith Communities*, Dr. Erik Carter notes, "We. What an incredible testimony it would be if the distinction between people with and without disabilities disappeared altogether in communities of faith. It could simply be *we* who engage in ministry, everyone together. When a congregation no longer thinks first and foremost along the lines of disability, it has probably arrived at its destination."[3]

Scripture also corrects our perspective quickly on the idea of an "all pink person." First Corinthians 12 addresses directly the false notion of one person being more or less gifted than another. We are gifted differently, and we all have gifts to share with others. Each part is important and critical to the body's functioning. God's knitting patterns are individually beautiful and different, and each person contains both green and pink stitches, including persons with an identified disability.

As it is, there are many parts, but one body. The eye cannot say to the hand, "I don't need you!" And the head cannot say to the feet, "I don't need you!" On the contrary, those parts of the body that seem to be weaker are indispensable, and the parts that we think are less honorable we treat with special honor. And the parts that are unpresentable are treated with special modesty, while our presentable parts need no special treatment. But God has put the body together, giving greater honor to the parts that lacked it, so that there should be no division in the body, but that its parts should have equal concern for each other. If one part suffers, every part suffers with it; if one part is honored, every part rejoices with it. (I Corinthians 12:20-26)

Let's allow that truth to settle in and change our vision and perspective. Can you think of someone in your life who has a disability? Think of that person's personality and the impact that person has on others. Describe some of the green stitches you notice

---

[3] Erik W. Carter, *Including People with Disabilities in Faith Communities: A Guide for Service Providers, Families, and Congregations* (Baltimore, MD: Paul H. Brookes, 2007)

in that person. Celebrate those areas of gifts and strengths. Thank God for those gifts present in your life through the life of that individual.

For persons reading this book who may feel like an "all pink person," allow God to speak truth to you. Whether you are "all pink" in your own perspective or those placed on you by another person or group of people, bathe yourself in the truth of Scripture. Know that you are an image bearer of God. Understand that you are God's dearly loved child. Be confident that God designed you with areas of gifting and wants to use those to impact the lives of others.

In his book *The Bondage Breaker*, Neil Anderson has a lengthy list of who we are in Christ. This list is based on words in Scripture and contains no asterisks. There is nothing in I Corinthians 12:27, for example, that says, "You are the body of Christ. Each one of you[*] is a part of it. [*Except for persons who may live with a physical or cognitive difference. *Except people who have trauma in their history. *Except people who are one particular gender or come from one particular culture.]" The statement stands on its own. Anderson's powerful list is a welcome addition to any refrigerator door or bathroom mirror, but here is a small part:

IN CHRIST, I Am Accepted.

John 1:12: I am God's child.

John 15:15: I am Christ's friend.

Romans 5:1: I have been justified.

I Corinthians 6:17: I am united with the Lord, and I am one spirit with Him.

I Corinthians 6:19, 20: I have been bought with a price. I belong to God.

1 Corinthians 12:27: I am a member of Christ's body. [4]

No asterisks!

The opposite, however, can also be true. Many of you reading this book may feel like you need to be an "all green person." Give yourself permission to see and admit the pinks in your stitching as well. For whatever reason, God's knitting pattern included both areas of strength and areas of challenge. I have wondered many times why God did not make my piece with more "greens"! How different my life would be if I could have been chosen first for the soccer team in fourth grade. Just winning one video game with those confounding controllers my sons had would have been lovely. Yet, how often do we expect ourselves to be all green, self-sufficient, gifted in all the ways needed within our communities? To expect too much green is to miss out on the next portion of the Scriptural perspective of puzzle pieces. The pieces fit together. We were designed to need one another.

Fitting Together in Community

Look back at the picture of the puzzle pieces all put together at the beginning of this chapter. God not only took time to hand-knit each individual, but then Scripture tells us that God arranges and places these individuals in communities. First Corinthians 12:18 reads, "But in fact God has placed the parts in the body, every one of them, just as he wanted them to be."

Our green and pink puzzle pieces are intended to fit together! God places us together, and we form a kind of giant "God body" puzzle. In

---

[4] Neil T. Anderson, *The Bondage Breaker: Overcoming Negative Thoughts, Irrational Feelings, Habitual Sins* (2000; repr. Eugene, OR: Harvest House, 2019), 54.

the places where I am strong, I can come alongside you. In the places where you are strong, you can come alongside me. We are truly designed to need one another – each one green and pink, giving to and receiving from one another. All Belong put together a three-minute video showing this idea through animation to help you reflect on this shift in thinking.[5]

Scripture is full of examples of partnerships and puzzle pieces fitting together. Already in Genesis 2:18, God notices Adam and says, "It is not good for the man to be alone. I will make a helper suitable for him." God created another puzzle piece to fit with Adam named Eve. Gifted and prominent Moses was noticing his own pinkness in the area of spoken words. God assigns a puzzle piece partner in his brother Aaron. In Exodus 4:16, God says to Moses, "He will speak to the people for you, and it will be as if he were your mouth."

Acknowledging the need for various puzzle pieces to function together comes out clearly in Acts 6. Since they had a need to continue teaching and preaching while also tending to the needs of the widows in the group, the disciples found a clear solution: intentionally look for specific areas of green in individuals and add them to the puzzle piece group: "So the Twelve . . . said . . . 'Brothers and sisters, choose seven men from among you who are known to be full of the Spirit and wisdom. We will turn this responsibility over to them and will give our attention to prayer and the ministry of the word.' This proposal pleased the whole group" (Acts 6:2–5). Scripture abounds with examples of the unique knitting patterns in individuals and how they fit

Certainly, we have modern-day examples of the puzzle piece community at work as well. Consider your own congregation. As we combine our puzzle pieces, it's clear that we depend on God to place

---

[5] "A Puzzle Piece Perspective," All Belong, April 22, 2021, https://vimeo.com/540229688.

people in our community who are teachers of children and teachers of adults. We call on those who have gifts of words or song, as well as those who bring joy or wonder to the community. We need those who have gifts of hospitality and creativity. Through the work of the Spirit, we bring ourselves to worship or a small group and end up receiving just what we needed from another member of the group. Sometimes we may know what we are lacking, and other times God sends what we need without our even being aware. Puzzle pieces fit together, and we count on God to create and place one another within that picture frame.

It makes sense, then, that we would be delighted to receive each one that God intends to place within our congregation. After all, how could we possibly know all that God has in store for us as individuals or for our life as a community? We would search for the gifts that person brings and be ready to support the areas of need. We would have intentional processes in place to make sure each puzzle piece can find a place of belonging within the larger group, as that person would certainly benefit the whole congregation.

3
Puzzle Piece Learning from Congregations

My friend, author Stephanie Hubach, says, "The church is uniquely equipped to come alongside families struggling for perspective."[6] So, what about Brandon? How could things have gone so wrong? Brandon was one of four children. He was born with a variety of physical and cognitive disabilities. Brandon and his family searched for five years to find a church where they could belong as a family. Each time, they were sent away with the words, "We don't have anything for him here." Or, "We're invested in another initiative right now and don't have the resources for that." Or, "Try the church down the road. We've heard they have a program for kids like him." Or, "We will clear out a room and you can come and watch him here on Sundays."

Each time, Brandon and his family went home, rejected from that community's puzzle. Brandon died at the age of five. His dad found a church down the road that was willing to allow the memorial service to happen there, but they would need to find a family friend to serve as the pastor for the event, since the leaders of the church did not know Brandon. The shocking reality is that the first time Brandon's body was welcome in a church was when it was lying in a casket. While his family got to know Brandon's greens and pinks, so many people lost out. Peers did not have the chance to befriend Brandon and learn some sign language to communicate together. Worshipers did not have the chance to see the giant smile that lit up his face when he was in the

---

[6] Stephanie O. Hubach, *Same Lake, Different Boat: Coming Alongside People Touched by Disability* (2006; repr., Phillipsburg, NJ: P&R, 2006), 132.

presence of worship music. Brandon and his family lost out, but so did the church community.

In a puzzle piece community, it should be unsettling when there is a missing piece—a gaping hole in the middle of the puzzle. People should be actively searching for that piece and making sure it fits so that the puzzle is complete. Yes, this is an example, one of many I have heard over the years, of communities that did not understand the puzzle piece perspective.

Thankfully, many congregations have this puzzle piece perspective. Brandon and his family would have been welcome in many other congregations. They would have been able to celebrate his life and mourn his death alongside his parents and siblings. They would have known about that giant smile during worship and would have known some of the signs Brandon knew when he communicated. They would have missed him when he was gone. They would have what Stephanie calls "interdependent unity [that] comes from diversity in the body of Christ." She notes that "everyone benefits when we choose intentional relationships with people of differing abilities."[7]

See what this looks like in the following scenarios.

Watermark Church in Grand Haven, Michigan, got a call from a mother of two adult sons with autism. She was struggling to find a place to worship. Her sons needed to have some space to move during worship and would need people to understand the backpack of items she takes along to help them stay calm and engaged during worship. The pastors got information from her, supplied her with details about the format of the worship service, and asked someone to meet the mom and her sons when they arrived. An area in the worship center where they would be comfortable to worship as a family was reserved,

---

[7] Hubach, *Same Lake, Different Boat*, 42.

and when their car arrived, the senior pastor scooted outside to greet the family and let them all know how glad the church was that they were there. What a different experience at Watermark! Brandon would have been known and loved in this place too.

In his book *I Choose Adam: Nothing Special Please*, Dr. David Winstrom reflects on his family's path on the way to finding a congregation that understood the puzzle piece perspective. While the Winstroms were ultimately able to settle into a Christian congregation, they initially found a Jewish temple that seemed to understand well who Adam was and how this baby with Down syndrome would be an important part of the community:

Jetta, Adam, and I only went a few times, but the Rabbi was right when he said, 'sit or walk during service, but just come and be part of community.' Sometimes Mary Beth would take Adam to church with her, but she said she never held Adam through the whole service because someone would always ask if they could please hold him. A community was affirming Adam. A community was wanting him to belong. A community was welcoming us, and it was not a program or technique; it was a fundamental knowing that all belong, and all are welcome. I learned that I will always be a good Jew first and then Christian. Jetta, Adam, and I were always welcomed and had an open invitation to come to Temple, parties, and gatherings. Good people found us. I began blessing Adam every Friday night, and I thanked Hashem for loaning me Adam, His perfect creation.[8]

Can you picture it? When a congregation can embrace the truth that each one of us is a combination of strengths and challenges and that each one of us is an important part of the body of Christ, the church community demonstrates a completely different perspective than a congregation that sees persons with disabilities as people to be

---

[8] David Winstrom, *I Choose Adam: Nothing Special Please* (Denver, CO: Lightning Tree Creative Media, 2017), 111.

pitied. The churches that rejected Brandon clearly did not see that the loss was not only to Brandon and his family. The gift that God had intended to impart to their community—that person who was to be placed there to grow the congregation in ways they had not yet discovered—was rejected. The church as a whole lost out when they sent Brandon away.

4
Puzzle Piece Take-Aways

Why is this puzzle piece perspective so important? Does it really make such a substantial difference to call this perspective "part 1 of the three-part plan" described in this book? Let me provide a few examples of how much a perspective forms our actions and interactions.

Transforming How We Talk

While trends change over time, an important concept right now is what is called "person-first language." In this way of speaking, it's important to note the person first and the type of disability second. Here are some examples:

Some May Say	Person First Language Says
Down syndrome boy	Boy with Down syndrome
Wheelchair bound Maria	Maria who is a wheelchair user
Schizophrenic	Person who lives with schizophrenia
Dementia patient	Someone living with dementia

Person-first language[9] is consistent with the puzzle piece perspective. It notices a *person* walking in the church door, a *person* in the hospital, or a *person* who comes over for dinner. While each individual mentioned lives with some form of disability, that is not the

---

[9] See allbelong.org for a Person First Language Guide, available in English and Spanish.

first thing mentioned. The focus is on *people first* and then on discovering the green and pink stitches that make up that person's life.

Charlotte vanOyen Witvliet writes:

[Keep] personhood primary. Language shapes the way we see and interact with each other and even how we see ourselves. Instead of referring to addicts or schizophrenics or anorexics or bulimics (as if diagnosis replaces personhood), we can speak of people who live with specific substance disorders, schizophrenia, or anorexia or bulimia, or people who are craving heroin, people who are who are hearing voices or who have disorganized speech, or people whose self-evaluation is overly influenced by their body shape or weight.[10]

For those speaking in front of others and preaching, praying, or making announcements, as well as for those preparing written materials such as bulletins, wall signs, or projection slides, person-first language is nearly always the best way of speaking. If you do develop a personal relationship with someone who has a disability, and that person prefers to be referred to as "an autistic," or "a disabled person" because it is a big part of that person's identity, certainly acknowledge that individual preference. That way of speaking, however, would be discovered within relationship.

Changing Our Prepositions

As I mentioned earlier, many of our congregations are tempted to build a ministry "can" and label it "ministry to people with disabilities." That may seem like the easiest or best option, but the puzzle piece perspective quickly points out that the use of the word to implies that the individual with a disability is a pink recipient and others are the green givers. Even switching the phrase to "ministry *for*

---

[10] Charlotte vanOyen Witvliet, "Speaking Well in Worship about Mental Illness," *Reformed Worship* 128 (June 2018): 14, www.reformedworship.org/article/june-2018/speaking-well-worship-about-mental-illnesses.

people with special needs" indicates a similar feel. You are pink, I am green, and I will give to you and expect nothing in return.

What if we had a "ministry *with* persons with disabilities"? What if we had an "accessible" opportunity? How can your church community allow members and visitors to know what you have available while also giving them a glimpse of the puzzle piece perspective?

Seeing Green

While it's possible to use our pink areas in God's service, it's important to acknowledge the green in each person. In fact, when we do so, we often ask questions differently. So often we focus on what a person *can't* do. Betsy can't talk, move her legs, or stay focused for longer than three minutes. Let me tell you, knowing what Betsy *can't* do will lead you to zero strategies to use when worshiping or learning together with Betsy. If you know, however, that she *can* use a device to communicate words and phrases she wants to say, *can* wave a streamer, or shake a tambourine, and *can* remember well what she sees in pictures, you now have the beginning of a way to worship, learn, and interact *with* Betsy.

When a child is part of a community and is born with an identified area of disability, the puzzle piece perspective allows us to speak with confidence about how God will grow the community through that person's presence. There is no question that this individual will have gifts to share as well as areas that will need the community's support. It can change conversations and the way we interact with family members and individuals.

Belonging, Not Just Inclusion

Have you ever labored hard to put together a jigsaw puzzle, only to find that a piece is missing? While the puzzle may have some lovely parts, the biggest eyesore is the missing piece! While some communities may believe that inclusion is the highest goal, it's not enough to set an individual puzzle piece on the table without truly fitting it into the completed whole. Puzzle pieces fit together, and to have a missing piece is a loss to the whole puzzle.

It's important that each God-designed green and pink piece has a spot within the whole. Some have said that inclusion is one thing, but when a person belongs, you miss them when they are gone. What a gift a community can provide to each of us! We fit in the puzzle, our contribution is important, and our absence leaves a gaping hole. We are missed.

In his book *Whole Community*, David Morstad says, "It has been suggested that there is a fundamental difference between the practice of inclusion and a true sense of belonging. Inclusion implies there is a group that decides to invite someone outside of itself to 'be included.' This is, by nature, a charitable act, an un-equal relationship. The message of inclusion is that we will make room for you. The message of belonging is that, if you're not here, we'll set out to go and find you, because we are not complete without you."[11]

Part 4 of this book offers many other ways this puzzle piece perspective comes alive in different ministries of our congregations.

---

[11] David Morstad, *Whole Community: Introducing Communities of Faith to People with Intellectual and Developmental Disabilities* (Bloomington, IN: Westbow, 2018), 83.

5
Reflections

While puzzle pieces are one way to think about God's design of individuals and community, Scripture provides many other themes and pictures to consider. As a special educator, I bring certain thoughts and gifts. I do not, however, have a background in theology. Therefore, I will display the gifting that God has given to two treasured colleagues and friends. They bring a research and theological perspective to this book that I have personally used in my devotional time during the preparation of this material. Combined with the puzzle piece perspective, these ideas provide us with a place to plant our feet as we move into the next part of our three-part plan: participation through universal design.

Biblical Themes to Guide Faith Communities That Seek to be Inclusive

By Dr. Thomas B. Hoeksema, Emeritus Professor, Calvin College

Congregations and parishes are motivated and shaped by biblically based principles. The foundational themes described here are intended to inspire and guide leaders and parishioners alike as they shape and implement ministry and community life that mirror the wide embrace of the One who loves us beyond measure.

Theme One: All Human Beings Embody the Image of the Creator God

The idea of being created in God's image is so familiar that we need to pause to unpack it within the context of human disability. None of us are perfect copies of God, yet we often value some people more than others. The notion of *imago Dei* (image of God; see Genesis 1:26) asserts that everyone in one way or another embodies some aspect of God. At the same time, we notice that human beings have many differences—in talent, temperament, appearance, intellectual ability, personality attributes, and in many other ways. Clearly, we are unique individuals, but we also are far more than our differences. And along with our differences, we are alike in that we are unfinished "works in progress." As Paul puts it in Colossians 3:10, we are being renewed into more perfect images of the Creator. That's true for all of us—both those who have been assigned disability labels and those who have not. Each of us is created by God and created in some ways to look like God and to accomplish God's purposes. We image God when we function as God's partners in renewing the world, and we image God when we partner with one another to extend God's love to the world.

Theme Two: Knowing That God Loves Us All Compels Response

God's lavish loving-kindness to us in choosing to become human in order to convince us we are loved cannot help but elicit gratitude in those who fully absorb this reality into their hearts and minds. Beyond our gratefulness, God wants his creatures to use faithfully whatever gifts the Creator God has given, regardless of how we might value or measure those gifts on some human scale (see Luke 21:1–4) and despite our "clay pot" imperfections, to accomplish his reign in the world. The call to love God and neighbor comes to every believer (Matthew 22:37–40). Each one of us, with all of our different capabilities and incapabilities, is God's instrument, carrying on God's work of reconciliation and restoration (see 1 Peter 4:10–11).

Theme Three: Unity Is God's Intent for the Family of God

In addition to bearing God's image and desiring to love God and neighbor, believers share a fundamental oneness. Despite individually unique embodiment of God's creativity (see 1 Corinthians 12:4), we are one because we share God's Spirit. Our level of intelligence, the acuity of our senses, and any impairment of bodily function are not obstacles to the Spirit's work in us. All of us can know God because the Spirit works in us in ways that are too mysterious for words and that go beyond intellect and verbalized faith. Believers have different gifts, but the same Spirit lives and breathes in us and through us.

As Paul reminds us several times in his epistles, we also are "one in Christ Jesus" (Galatians 3:28). For all of us—bound and free, female and male, African and European, those who speak with their tongues and those who speak with their hands, those who experience disability and those who are temporarily able-bodied—Christ has broken down the barriers that divide us from one another (see Ephesians 2:14–18). All of us are members of God's household—those who "are being built together to become a dwelling in which God lives by his Spirit" (2:22).

Theme Four: We Give and Receive Compassion

In both the Old and New Testaments, Scripture calls us to extend compassionate care to the widow, the orphan, those who are poor, the displaced, and anyone who is in need. Much of the church's early involvement with people who had disabilities was motivated by a deep sense of care. That is well and good.

Often overlooked, however, is that compassion can and even should be an experience of mutuality. It is not just a matter of the strong caring for the weak. Compassion involves giving and receiving simultaneously—for *everyone* involved. This is not the familiar, "I get way more out of this than I give." God's people must open themselves to receiving compassion, as well as look for opportunities to offer it.

Many who have relationships with people who too often are only viewed as needing compassion and care find themselves the delighted recipients of caring compassion. As they become known, including their own burdens and needs, people who begin relationships as caregivers may find themselves being cared for by their friend. It is important to realize that receiving and giving care offers gifts to both the giver and receiver. Receiving care thankfully is a gift back to the giver and rewards both persons. In the mutual sharing of joys and burdens, people receive in their giving and give in their receiving.

Theme Five: In God's family We Experience Interdependence and Reciprocity

God's design is for people to use their diversity to serve each other and to serve in partnership with each other. Human diversity is part of the creation order; it's the way God intends things to be. Our ableist world defines people by particular capabilities and incapabilities. People who are labeled according to some perceived disability typically are seen as dependent on others and as relatively passive recipients of other people's generosity. However, if each person is created with purpose, it must mean that each one is "necessary" (1 Corinthians 12:27 TLB). Persons called "disabled" and those mistakenly called "nondisabled" all contribute who they are to the welfare of the body (see Romans 12:3–8; Ephesians 4:16). In fact, without everyone's gifts, the body of believers could not do all the things God asks them to do. Not one of us can do all of God's work without the other members of the community. You could say we image God together; collectively, we form a body that carries more of God's image. We are not only God's covenant partners in a vertical relationship; we also are covenant partners, horizontally, with one another. God's household is a web of partnerships between people, all of whom are a mix of strength and weakness, gift and need (see 2 Corinthians 12:7–10). Equally broken (see 1 John 1), we also are equally called to be servants of and with each other (see Philippians 2).

Theme Six: We Exercise Hospitality

Hospitality, in part, is the practice of welcoming "the other," and it is the polar opposite of exclusion.

Like many other types of strangers, people with disabilities are often unfamiliar to members of our faith communities. They may be viewed as strange and are perhaps avoided and isolated because of their perceived differences. They do not feel like they belong; and when they are not there, sadly, they are often not missed.

In Scripture, we find ample testimony to the centrality of the virtue of hospitality. In the Old Testament, entire cities became places of refuge, and God is described as loving the foreigner (see Deuteronomy 10:18). In the New Testament, Jesus provides the model of the master inviting unexpected guests—strangers—to the great feast (see Luke 14:16–24). Making people feel that they belong is an integral part of what it means to be God's family.

Hospitality is deeper than graciously welcoming people and making them feel like they belong. It is not about eradicating difference, assimilating the stranger by making the other be like oneself. Rather, hospitality requires and capitalizes on differentness. It overcomes fear of the stranger and instead celebrates oneness with the other alongside of, or in the middle of, human differences. As with compassion, an element of mutuality is involved. Hospitality creates space within oneself for what the other has to offer. In this way, a community fulfills God's command to love our neighbor as ourselves (see Luke 10:26–28) and foreshadows the heavenly banquet in which each one of us, with all of our distinctive imperfections, is invited in as guests. How unexpected!

Conclusion

These six themes interact and are not perfectly discrete. They are woven together like strands in a cord, creating a tapestry that reveals something of the shalom, the peace and well-being, that God wants us to experience in our lives together.

In the 1980s, early leaders in "disability ministry" began talking about "ministry *with*" rather than "ministry *to*" persons with disabilities. Many churches do not yet understand the difference between providing services to people with disabilities and preparing communities to receive what people with disabilities have to offer. To "minister *with*," churches need to consider how they unwittingly may have contributed to the marginalization of people with disabilities. And they need to discover how to receive the ministry offered by our sisters and brothers who live with disability.

Doing this work will renew the church. It is a work of reconciliation. By reconciling people both with and without labeled disabilities, the church can be transformed into an inclusive fellowship where strangers of any type—returning citizens (ex-offenders), gender minorities, substance abusers, those experiencing homelessness or insecurity in a source of food, those estranged for whatever reason—can all experience belonging and a warm embrace.

As we have noted, there is much reciprocity in this work. We not only are offering grace, but are receiving the grace channeled through others, including people who are given labels. The spirit of gracious hospitality renews the entire church by embodying the astounding depth and wideness of God's mercy and love.

The church is beginning to recognize that the presence and contributions of those whom the world has viewed as "the least of these" and as "weak" or "foolish" are central to its identity. More members of faith communities are willing to be taught by and healed by those whom they previously have viewed only as needy. People with disabilities embody the wisdom of God in ways that can be prophetic. As Henri Nouwen and Jean Vanier have shown us, people with profound disability are our teachers. Amos Yong, in his book

Theology and Down Syndrome, puts it this way: "Disabilities qualify rather than disqualify people for Christian ministry."[12]

God is making all things new, and you can be a part of it.

For the Joy Set before Us: Biblical Themes to Sustain Our Ministry of Mutuality over a Lifetime

By Dr. John D. Witvliet, Director of the Calvin Institute of Christian Worship and Professor of Worship, Theology, and Congregational and Ministry Studies

Let's begin with the vision that Professor Hoeksema described so compellingly:

- All human beings embody the image of God.
- Knowing God's love for all of us compels response.
- Unity is God's intent for his family.
- We are graced when we both give and receive compassion.
- In God's family, we experience interdependence and reciprocity.
- In God's family, mutual hospitality is a joy, not a burden.

Each of these themes are foundational to a vision for mutuality. Part of our challenge is that even when we agree with something, it doesn't always sink deeply into our hearts. And even when we as believers assent to this vision, we don't always live by it. The roots of this vision aren't always planted as deeply as they need to be in our hearts. What can we do to let this sink deeply into our hearts? What can sustain our lifelong engagement with these foundational themes?

---

[12] Amos Yong, *Theology and Down Syndrome: Reimagining Disability in Late Modernity* (Waco, TX: Baylor University Press, 2007), 218.

Word Pictures

One means the Holy Spirit uses to deepen these roots within us is through our practices of meditation on Scripture. One of the gifts of the Bible is that it gives us so many different word pictures—so many different images or metaphors—for helping us grasp this vision. These are word pictures to ponder, to think through, and to savor. And these word pictures offer us more than just ideas to think about. Part of what they convey is the beauty—compelling splendor, loveliness, and attractiveness—of this vision of the church.

So, as you return to Professor Hoeksema's core themes, hopefully repeatedly, consider beginning your study each time by dwelling for a while with one of the core word pictures that the Bible uses to describe the church. Each image invites us into surprising discoveries.

- Picture Christian community like *a body* (Romans 12; 1 Corinthians 12; Ephesians 4:12), with its many members and parts. What a vivid picture of interdependence this is!
- Picture Christian community like *a temple* (1 Corinthians 3:16), a gathering of "living stones" (2 Peter 5)—a beautifully ordered building designed to be the habitation for God's Holy Spirit. What a vivid picture this is of how the Holy Spirit indwells us!
- Picture Christian community like *a garden or field*, where "God gives the growth" (1 Corinthians 3:9).
- Picture Christian community like a *vine*, where each of are like branches grafted into Christ, the vine (John 15:5), who bear the fruit of the Spirit (Galatians 5:22–23).
- Picture Christian community like *a procession* (Isaiah 60:1–9, Revelation 21:24), a parade of God-fearing people bringing gifts and treasure into the kingdom of God.
- Picture Christian community like a *sheepfold*, where we all are sheep cared for by the Good Shepherd, and where the Good Shepherd goes out from the fold to seek lost sheep (John 10).

In each case, pause to ask, "How do this word picture deepen our vision? How does this word picture deepen our feelings about this vision? What new or surprising insights come from this word picture?"

Puzzle Piece Theology

The Bible also commissions us within the Christian community to be effective teachers and advocates for vibrant interdependent communities of hospitality and mutual ministry. Effective teaching often happens when we develop additional faithful and instructive word pictures to convey a vision and invite people to new moments of insight.

Barb Newman's "puzzle piece" word picture is a compelling example. It is simple and memorable, and it beautifully conveys so many different biblical themes at once.

- Just like a puzzle piece is incomplete by itself, so are we as individuals incomplete without others.
- Just like a puzzle piece is carefully designed so that it fits together with others, so are we designed to fit together with others. We are created for relationship.
- Just as puzzle pieces can come in all sorts of shapes, with every possible design of its corners and edges, so too we human beings come with such a wide variety of gifts and personalities.
- Just as an individual puzzle piece may well have something that seems at first to be out of place until it is set within the whole puzzle, so too it is the whole Christian community that helps us see the beauty and uniqueness of each individual member.
- Just like one missing puzzle piece in an otherwise complete puzzle sends us on a passionate search for the missing piece, so too we should passionately seek out those puzzle pieces

who are not yet a part of Christian community—often because we haven't welcomed them. This reminds us of how Jesus as the Good Shepherd actively seeks the lost sheep (see John 10).
- Just like a puzzle, when fully assembled, can convey a beautiful, compelling, or surprising picture, so too we as a Christian community are called to convey to the world a beautiful, compelling, and surprising vision of goodness.

Of course, not every aspect of every word picture is a perfect comparison. In puzzles, each piece may only fit with an exact match. In Christian community, each of us fits beautifully with all kinds of different people. In puzzles, each piece is static. Unlike bodies and vines, puzzles are inanimate. In Christian community, we are each dynamic—ever growing in our capacity to fit together with others in Christ's service. Still, mindful of these points of divergence, there is so much to gain from this instructive image.

Praise Sets the Tone

As we continue to live with this biblical vision over time and as we become more fervent advocates for inclusion and justice, one of the key questions we need to ask ourselves is this: "Are our advocacy and passion continually grounded in our praise of God?"

At first, that may seem unusual. Prophetic advocacy is typically associated with sorrow—even anger—at injustice and lack of inclusion. But that sorrow and righteous anger always point to something deeper, to the stunningly beautiful vision of what is good, right, and true that helps us discern what is wrong. As C. S. Lewis once noted, we don't know what is crooked until we know first what a straight line is, and we don't know how to tell what injustice is until we see a vision of pure and perfect justice.[13]

---

[13] See C. S. Lewis, *Mere Christianity* (1943; repr., New York: Macmillan, 1969), 45–46.

When we glimpse the glory, beauty, justice, and perfect relationality of the triune God, perfectly revealed in Jesus, we offer praise. The triune God is the perfect picture of unity and mutuality (see John 17). God's commands to practice mutuality and hospitality are altogether beautiful, renewing the soul. When we contemplate, savor, and praise God for these remarkably beautiful dimensions of God's own character, our own moral compasses are sharpened.

This also changes the tone of our advocacy. We advocate for inclusion for the joy set before us (see Hebrews 12:2). We advocate as eager, buoyant believers who have grasped—or have been grasped by—a stunning vision. It excites us so much that we would, having discovered a treasure, eagerly sell our possessions in order to buy the field where that treasure is hidden (see Matthew 13:44). At times, convicted joy about this vision will lead us to be prophetic in our expression of frustration, even anger, at examples of inhospitality. But ultimately, that frustration and righteous anger is not the tone that defines us. The tone is set by our wonder and praise of a God who shows us a better way.

God's Agency and Our Joy

As we continue to become more fervent advocates for inclusion and justice, we can become weary. The roadblocks and barriers can be significant. And then we need to recall that, ultimately, communities of healthy mutuality, inclusiveness, hospitality, and mutual ministry are gifts of the Holy Spirit. It is the Holy Spirit who works—often imperceptibly—to orchestrate the beautiful exchange of gifts in Christian community.

That does not mean we are passive. The Holy Spirit gifts each of us, calls each of us, prompts each of us to be active in our obedience and mutual love toward this vision.

But it is not as if the Holy Spirit then leaves us on our own—to engage in all of this on our own strength. And it is not as if we can say, "Well, we did about half of this, and the Spirit did the other half." That is not how the mathematics of the Holy Spirit works! Rather, after we are justified through Jesus Christ (100 percent God's work, 0 percent human work), then the Holy Spirit so often heals, equips, calls, strengthens, and works through human agency—in persons across the spectrum of ability and disability—so that what is accomplished in Jesus 'name is more like 100 percent God's work, 100 percent our work. That's the doctrine of sanctification—the work of the Spirit within and among us.

How remarkable it is that Scripture would invite us to picture ourselves as walking "in step with the Spirit" (Galatians 5:25) or being "hidden with Christ in God" (Colossians 3:3).

How remarkable that Scripture would picture those who call others to live out kingdom values as "Christ's ambassadors, as though God were making his appeal through us" (2 Corinthians 5:20), or as "co-workers in God's service" (1 Corinthians 3:9).

How remarkable that Scripture would depict believers as "living stones" being built up into a temple where God dwells (1 Peter 2:5), or like fruit-bearing branches being grafted into Christ the vine (see John 15:5; Galatians 5:22–23)—images that portray God's power and agency at work not only in the context around us, but also within and through us.

How remarkable it is to see all the Scripture texts that display this interweaving of God's action and ours:

- "In their hearts humans plan their course, but the Lord establishes their steps" (Proverbs 16:9).

- "Work out your salvation in fear and trembling, for it is God who works in you to will and to act in order to fulfill his good purpose" (Philippians 2:12-13)
- "I worked harder than all of them—yet not I, but the grace of God that was within me" (1 Corinthians 15:10); "I planted the seed, Apollos watered it, but God has been making it grow" (1 Corinthians 3:6).
- "Be transformed [passive] by the renewing of your mind [active]" (Romans 12:2).
- "As you come to him, the living Stone [active] . . . you also, like living stones, are being built [passive] into a spiritual house" (1 Peter 2:4).

Every one of these texts is an invitation to prayer: "Lord, may our advocacy, our planning, our giving, our working toward this vision of inclusion be a participation in your great work. Send your Holy Spirit to us. Help us walk in step with your Spirit each step of the way."

And in this, too, there is great joy. The fruitfulness of inclusive community is not ultimately something we heroically accomplish on our own. We do this work together, embedded in the larger purposes of God and in the strength and power the Holy Spirit provides.

6
Practical Tools for Your Congregation

Useful for distributing puzzle piece perspective in your congregation, with people of all ages.

1: Puzzle Piece Lesson Plan

Build your own green and pink puzzle piece wall display. A simplified lesson based on something All Belong has used for years is provided here which you can use to create your own visual example of community. Try it in youth group, adult small group, children's setting, staff/volunteer training, or large group setting. It works best if everyone present has access to their own puzzle piece to design.

Introduce the Idea of Puzzle Pieces

Play the puzzle piece animation video from All Belong or share with the group, "The Bible tells us in Psalm 139:13 that God knit us together before we were even born. He created us and had a plan for us from the moment we were conceived. Each person in the group gathered today has a page in God's pattern book." As you hold up a green and pink puzzle piece, discuss with the group the idea of strengths and weaknesses. Say, "Part of God's pattern is that we all have things that are easy for us and things that are difficult for us. It's part of God's plan. We have green parts—areas of strength. Green stands for growth and strength. We also have pink parts— areas of weakness and challenge. Pink stands for hot spots or things that are difficult."

Lead by Example

Talk about your own puzzle piece (feel free to make your piece ahead of time). Talk about areas that are easy for you and things that are more difficult. As you discuss your own puzzle piece, it will help others begin to form their own ideas.

Engage the Group

Give each person a puzzle piece that is half green and half pink. Ask each participant to add two or three words on the green side to represent their areas of strength and one or two words on the pink side to represent areas of need or challenge.

Put It All Together

Using some sort of adhesive, connect the puzzle pieces to form a wall display. These can either be in one long line or in a square or rectangular formation. If you did not view the video, you can share with the group that "God made us on purpose to fit together. He calls us one body. If I was "all green," I would not need any other people. I could fix the broken furnace, mow the lawn, decorate the building, write the newsletter, preach a sermon, teach a class, make a meal for someone who is sick, and watch all of the children in the nursery. I would not need anyone else. That's *not* how God made us. He made us to fit together like a puzzle (demonstrate with some of their pieces). Where _____ [insert person's name] is strong, that person can help someone else. Where _____ [insert person's name] is weak, another one can come alongside and help that person. It's part of God's design for His church. When we give our life to Jesus, we give Him our entire puzzle piece. He gets the green and the pink. With our life in His hands, He can use it all. Sometimes God uses our areas of challenge in His service as well as things that are easy for us. He also loves our entire puzzle piece. He treasures you as a person, not for what you can or cannot do."

While the display is going up, or when it is complete, read 1 Corinthians 12:14–20 together.

2: True-False Quiz

A quick way to get information into the hands of a community is through a variation of the true-false quiz used earlier in this chapter. Consider using some of these questions or research some of your own. By asking people to respond with thumbs-up for true and thumbs-down for false, it allows the participants to actively be engaged with the questions and content. The questions and answers are a fun way to get some valuable information to your congregation.

3: Small Group Learning Ideas

As you put together your learning opportunities in adult education or leadership training, consider using the following ideas:

- Read and discuss the theological perspective written by Dr. Thomas Hoeksema Sr. and Dr. John Witvliet.

- Compare and discuss two diverse perspectives. View the two videos below and discuss what each video says about that community's view of a person and of a community. What evidence do you see of a puzzle piece perspective? If that is not evident, what perspective does each video convey?

    o "Worship as One: Disability in Community," which captures practices and thoughts from three different congregations.[14]

---

[14] "Worship as One: Disability in Community (video)," *Worship as One* online resources, see links at https://allbelong.org/worship-as-one.

- o A documentary about a former residential facility on Staten Island called Willowbrook. While this video is about a half hour, the first twelve minutes should give you enough to discuss as a group.[15]

- Dan Vander Plaats at Elim Christian Services provides excellent materials. You can download a copy of the *5 Stages: The Journey of Disability Attitudes*.[16] This one-page document allows a congregation to think through stages of ignorance, pity, care, friendship, and co-laborers. Imagine your congregation, as well as your own perspective, on a journey to the puzzle piece perspective.

- To use in a children's setting or intergenerational group (or at a school chapel or for devotions as a family), consider picking up a copy of the book *Body Building* by Barbara J. Newman.[17] I wrote this book to celebrate the gifts that persons with disabilities bring to our church and school communities.

---

[15] "Willowbrook: The Last Great Disgrace (Full 1972 Special)," ABC7NY, Eyewitness News, posted April 1, 2022, https://abc7ny.com/11700456.
[16] College, Wheaton. "Stages of Attitudes." Wheaton College, https://www.wheaton.edu/wheaton-center-for-faith-and-disability/disability-foundations/stages-of-attitudes/. Accessed 4 Nov. 2022.
[17] Barbara J. Newman, *Body Building: Devotions to Celebrate Inclusive Community* (Wyoming, MI: Christian Learning Center, 2009).

Part 2
Participation: Universal Design

Defining Universal Design

Universal Design is a way of designing buildings, products, and environments that make them accessible to all people, with and without disabilities.

7

Introduction to Participation: Universal Design

Let's examine the church welcome sign. "Everyone welcome" is clearly posted on the door leading to where you worship as a congregation. Sometimes, however, I imagine seeing several other signs beside that one. They may not be posted but imagine if it could be true of your worship setting.

> **WARNING:**
> - ✓ Must be able to read
> - ✓ Must be able to speak
> - ✓ Must be able to write
> - ✓ Must be able to read a musical score
> - ✓ Must be able to focus and pay attention to a primarily word-based lecture for at least 20 minutes while staying seated and quiet
> - ✓ Must be primarily an auditory learner
> - ✓ Must be able to stand, sit, and kneel on command
> - ✓ Must be comfortable shaking hands and greeting others
> - ✓ Must be able to tolerate the smell of various perfumes, deodorants, after-shaves, and hairsprays

Clearly, we could add several more to this list. For a person unable to do one or more of these items, participation may be limited in a worship setting. It's also possible that these kinds of signs could be posted on the doorways of children's ministry, youth group, adult small groups, and fellowship areas.

But how does a congregation put together opportunities without tapping into some of these skill areas? How can persons with varied abilities be more welcome? Can we rip down some of those extra signs so that the "everyone welcome" sign is the most prominent one?

My enthusiastic answer is, *Yes!* In fact, I am thrilled to introduce you to the concept that is key to participation—namely, universal design. Universal design was originally introduced through the work of architects. That work has then been imported into many other settings, including classrooms and educational settings. The possibility, therefore, for congregations to use this idea opens doors to tearing down the walls that many of the statements mentioned above erect.

Architects design buildings with multiple options. They create buildings in the expectation that persons of varied abilities will use that space. Their design typically includes stairs to various building levels, as well as elevators or ramps. The parking lots have designated areas for those who need to park close to the entrance. There are curb cuts, bathrooms designed for a variety of users, braille on the walls, and hearing loops or other accommodations built in. Width and height are factored into much of the space. Buildings are created with multiple options for those who will use it.

The architect may not have met anyone who will need the accessible features prior to creating the building, but there is a certainty that the features are important and will be used by many.

Universal design is different from accessible design. The word *universal* applies not only to the 20 to 25 percent of the population that lives with some sort of disability; that word reveals that the features will benefit *all of us* during different ages and stages of life. It's intended for 100 percent of the community. For example, if your hands are totally full and you come to a door with an automatic door opener, will you push that button clearly labeled with a wheelchair symbol to get inside hands-free? Do you happen to have a garage door opener in your car? Did you know it was created for people who have limited mobility? Aren't you glad you have one? Are you a person who typically walks unassisted but suffered an injury that affected your mobility, and you now find yourself thankful for elevators and nearby parking spaces? Has the aging process resulted in your benefiting from the hearing loop that interacts with your hearing aid at an event you're attending? Do you enjoy a large-print version of a magazine or menu so you don't have to grab your reading glasses just to make out the words?

Having learned important lessons from the universal design idea that focuses on physical design, educators have applied the "multiple option" idea to learning settings—a concept known as "universal design for learning. Educators are expecting children of varied abilities to be part of classrooms. Some students learn best through words and others learn best through pictures. Both options, therefore, are built into the lesson from the beginning.

How do learners take information in and how do they get information out? Written words may work for some as they "show what they know," but that may not be true for all learners. There may be options to use written words, spoken words, videos, or a display. By adding options, it becomes easier to include children of varied abilities in a more complete way. Participation improves, increases, and becomes more meaningful. The entire group has options that are built-in right at the lesson planning stage.

Architects build buildings in the expectation that people of all abilities will use that space. Educators build lesson plans in the expectation that students of all abilities will be part of the classroom setting. Could it be that congregations will be motivated to build its ministries in the expectation that people of all abilities will be part of their settings?

What would it look like to have our congregations build children and youth programming, corporate worship services, adult small group Bible studies, Wednesday evening potlucks, outreach projects, and other offerings expecting people of all abilities to be part of those settings?

Congregations that adopt universal design principles will build in options and supports for people of all abilities throughout the planning process. The planning process may be on a large scale, such as a building renovation or remodeling project, but the process also happens on a small scale, such as planning for a weekly worship service or preparing for a children's ministry event.

Not only will universal design principles help shape the spaces where people gather so that they are accessible to all, options and supports will be built into the learning and activities the congregation offers. Church leaders, committee members, volunteers, and attendees will actively participate in creating environments that are carefully crafted to include 100 percent of those who gather. Congregations will be aware of the unintended signs that can cover up the "Everyone Welcome" sign and actively work to eliminate any obstacles that stand in the way of true belonging.

Delighting in the Possibilities for Congregations

I am a huge fan of universal design for congregations. Many churches respond to the goal of welcoming persons with varied abilities through the making of personalized plans for individuals who need any form of support. Certainly, that is an important part of a congregational plan (and one we'll discuss in the next chapter about responsive design), but so many miss out on the delight of thinking about participation and universal design. We can identify many reasons why focusing on universal design makes sense in a congregation. Let me name a few.

You can prepare in advance. You don't have to wait for an individual to show up or voice a need. Congregations can assume persons with varied abilities will be part of each setting. Begin to choose some items and put them in place. Every ministry area in the church can add universal design to their meeting agenda. What can we provide to increase options while limiting the number of unwanted and unintended signs at our ministry or event doors that hide the welcome sign from view? Remember, a good disability ministry is a lot more like shredded cheese than a stand-alone can. Shredded cheese is sprinkled through the entire congregational recipe, and universal design helps each portion of the church be more accessible to a greater number of people.

The right people oversee options. So often a congregation taps a person or committee to take the lead in creating a welcome place of belonging for persons with disabilities. While such a person or committee can play a vital role, as I'll suggest later, many other leaders in the church are quick to pass the baton to that person or committee. Here is the problem with that model when it comes to universal design. If, for example, the preacher for the day "owns" both the content of the message and the concept of universal design, they will be able to plant the right visual, create the right "big idea," and plan a movement break within the message as needed because that person best knows the content of the message. If the "disability coordinator" was in charge of making this happen, they may not have the expertise in preaching, and the preacher may not like the ideas or be comfortable with the delivery. The preacher knows how to preach. The worship leader knows worship. The children's teacher knows how to interact with children. The custodian knows what the best products are for cleaning. The office support staff knows how to create documents. If these natural leaders with giftings in these areas understand some basic principles for universal design, these people are best equipped to choose and implement what makes sense within their areas. Given the information about people's sensory differences and aversions to certain smells, the custodian can choose the right products for cleaning the church. Given information about the importance of large-print resources and how to achieve that, the office support staff can make sure a large-print handout exists for every gathering.

To have one person or a committee be aware of and promote person-first language is great, but to have those who hold the microphone each week practice it will transform your community much more quickly. Natural leaders "own" their areas, and the responsibility to implement universal design features in that area should belong to that individual. Look into the "Utilize Best Practices" section at the end of this chapter for examples and links to help you think about the various roles in the church and how each role can be versed in universal design.

The impact is not just for the 20 percent; it's for the 100 percent. True to the name, universal design is for *all* those who gather. The term *varied abilities* applies to all of us. While it's important to think specifically about community belonging and persons with disabilities, the options put in place through universal design are intended to impact a much larger number of people.

Take, for example, a pastor who decides that each week the message will be accompanied by an object hidden in a treasure chest. At some point during the message, that object will be revealed and will clearly illustrate the big idea of the message from Scripture. How many people will learn and remember that point more clearly with a much-anticipated item hidden away and revealed to the group? I would contend that more than 80 percent of those gathered will appreciate that feature. Children in particular may look forward to that unveiling each week. If your community includes persons who are not fluent in the language used in the oral presentation, that person has an important link to the message. If you are a learner who remembers best when a visual is used, you will appreciate it too. Visuals are often important for persons living with dementia as well. And if a person has tuned out for some of the message, a visual is a wonderful way to bring them back into the experience. What's more, if the visual is an object that someone can touch and feel, this may be a great benefit for a person who has limited or no vision. And with all this, we may have just exceeded the 80 percent mark and are now soaring to at least 90 percent of your congregation. The effort you put in impacts all members of your community in a positive way. Best said, universal design for a physical space and universal design for learning is a great "bang for your buck" in terms of time, energy and resources invested.

A focus on universal design decreases the demand for personalized plans. Personalized plans are still important and make up the third strand in this three-part plan. The reality is that they can take time and energy to put together. Furthermore, they often single people out, as in "this is Ally's plan." Ally may indeed need a specific plan; however, it's also possible that a children's ministry set up according to principles of universal design can eliminate the need for a personalized plan. Perhaps the leaders have stocked each children's meeting area with a few options for children who need to have regular movement to focus and concentrate. If that leader has been equipped to understand how to use a fidget pencil or a wiggle cushion or knows when to offer options to sit on the floor, in a rocking chair, or stand for the telling of the Bible story, then Ally's need for movement can simply be part of "standard equipment and procedures" that are routinely available in that setting. The leaders may be surprised how many other children will take advantage of that equipment as well. Plus, if a parent knows that Ally needs this equipment to be successful and they see multiple rooms with these items, it's delightful to see how this equipment can speak a word of hospitality to Ally and her parents. These items call out, "We were expecting you. You are welcome here. We've got this covered."

We will explore this further in the "Responsive Design" section, but it's worth noting here the work of Dr. María Cornou (program manager for international and intercultural learning for the Calvin Institute of Christian Worship) that supports the idea that highlighting universal design better welcomes families for whom a personalized plan may be culturally difficult to receive.[18]

You can start small or big. Another excellent feature of universal design is that you can choose options that make sense for your community. If this concept is completely new to your congregation, you may want to choose three or four ideas that make sense. Perhaps you will decide to offer a gluten-free choice during the Lord's Supper, alter your "please stand" invitation to "please rise in body or in spirit," and offer a large-print option for your handouts, bulletins, and newsletters. Start there and add more pieces to your universal design plan as you become comfortable with the concept.

Perhaps you'll begin your focus in the worship area or the youth group area and then let it filter to other places. Perhaps your congregation already sees a big benefit to this. You may want to schedule a retreat or a leadership day when you carefully examine your areas of oversight and decide which specific options you may want to implement. See the practical ideas shared at the end of this chapter for resources to guide that process. Plan, implement, and then evaluate after a few months. What do you want to alter, add, or delete to the plan? Your implementation of universal design principles can be totally individualized to the comfort and calling of your congregation.

---

[18] María Cornou, "Universal Design for Worship: Consider Cultural Differences," shared at an event (Renovate Church: Creating a Space for All Abilities) in Bothell, Washington, October 24, 2018.

8
Learning from Congregations Using Universal Design

I have the honor of introducing you to some congregations that have purposefully thought about and implemented the universal design vision so you can get a sampling of what it can look like. If you are excited to see universal design in other settings in the church, you can flip ahead to part 4 to find more stories.

Universal Design Options and Children's Settings

In the introduction to their book *Every Child Welcome*, Katie Wetherbee and Jolene Philo point out, "Jesus sets a high standard in Matthew 19:14 when He says, 'Let the little children come to me and do not hinder them, for to such belongs the kingdom of heaven.' His invitation is inclusive. No gender is specified. The call is not limited to children who will sit quietly at His feet and listen, color between the lines, raise their hands and wait to be called upon, or who work at grade level. No child is disqualified because of preexisting physical conditions, mental illness, or behavior issues."[19]

One terrific way to get ready to open your arms for each child is to think through and implement the idea of universal design. Children's ministry is one of the places a congregation sees clearly that children come to a church setting with varied abilities!

While speaking at Memorial Road Church in Edmond, Oklahoma, I had a chance to see notable features of universal design built into their children's ministry. First, the church invested in their volunteers

---

[19] Katie Wetherbee and Jolene Philo, *Every Child Welcome: A Ministry Handbook for Including Kids with Special Needs* (Grand Rapids: Kregel Academic, 2015), 9.

by providing training in this area. I was part of that learning and equipping by being invited to their community. We spent time looking at some of the equipment and tools one could use within the context of a Sunday school setting to best welcome children of varied abilities. The volunteers left with an arsenal of tools to try on Sunday. They also decided to stock many of those items as standard supplies. Not only did the individual meeting rooms have fidgets and varied seating options, but they also had multiple leaders, so they could address individual and small group needs within that setting. The church had also recently made a special sensory room for children who needed a break or a spot to regroup from the onslaught of sensation so often part of children's ministry. This room was well designed with soft lighting, tactile activities, calming sound level, and movement options. It was well researched and well designed. Although a recent add-on, the children's area also was now accessible through an elevator. Looking to the future, they knew it would be important to have this option for those children yet to come.

Universal Design options and Worship Settings

While worship happens in children, adult, and intergenerational settings, my examples here will focus on the large-group corporate worship setting.

Saint Andrew's Presbyterian Church in Iowa City, Iowa, was about to move into their new building when I was invited to be part of a training weekend. It was clear as the pastor gave me a tour of the new facility that the community embraced the idea of universal design. Not only was the worship area equipped with a hearing loop and significant effort had been put into being able to control sound levels for those in attendance, but they had also planned to create flexible meeting areas, some small and some large. The option would be provided for someone to attend worship and spend time in a small and intimate area with the ability to adjust the sound. Other people could worship in a larger area where an amazing pipe organ was a prominent part of that community. They had taken into consideration both those who walked into the building and those who rolled in. They had taken into consideration individuals who are introverts and those who are extroverts. The spacious setting would physically and "educationally" welcome a wide range of individuals.

It was not, however, only the *new* space that was the target of intentional planning to welcome persons of all abilities. Their *existing* space was also well planned. They made intentional use of my time to cast the puzzle piece perspective to the congregation as a whole. The community was equipped and expecting persons with varied abilities. When I looked around during morning worship, it was clear that the presence of some individuals who were wheelchair users, adults and children with Down syndrome, and people who were English language learners all had a place of belonging within that community. Their presence was not unique or "special;" it was simply "normal" to have a community made up of persons with varied abilities who worshiped together. This congregation were excited to use the gifts and support the challenges of all gathered.

Another congregation that spent considerable time thinking about universal design is Fairway Christian Reformed Church in Jenison, Michigan. The community requested training in autism spectrum disorder, so All Belong had the opportunity to see how much time they had already spent on universal design principles.

First, they wanted to equip their congregation with more understanding about autism spectrum disorder. Continuing to learn and grow in our understanding of one another is crucial. In addition to that, I was greeted by a team of people in the winter who offered valet parking. People who wanted to avoid walking through an icy parking lot could pull up to the door and allow someone else to park their car. A note in the bulletin indicated that noise-cancelling headphones for anyone who needed them were available at a specific counter for checkout.

At the time of my visit, a trip to their website (www.fairwaycrc.org) revealed that they were working hard at communicating a welcome to those with varied abilities. This quote was included in their reflections on their opening page:

"We have three different environments to help you worship in the way you're most comfortable:

- a traditional-style worship in our sanctuary
- a casual worship experience around tables in our Great Room
- a quiet and calm worship space with alternative seating options in our sensory worship room

Anyone with a name tag can help you find the choice where you'd be most comfortable.

Our building is barrier-free. All are welcome to participate fully in the life of our church!"[20]

Do you see how clear it is that these churches are expecting persons of varied abilities to be part of worship each Sunday? These options are built-in and always available. I will go into greater detail about worship settings in part 4, but I hope these examples provide a taste of universal design principles and implementation and the worship practices of two congregations that understand the value of investing time and energy into providing options to all who gather.

---

[20] See Mark Stephenson, "Five Ideas for Creating Belonging," CRC Network, June 17, 2019, https://network.crcna.org/disability-concerns/5-ideas-belonging.

9

Practical Tools for Your Congregation:

Useful for implementing Universal Design in your congregation.

1: Drama

One way to give your congregation a taste of the importance of universal design is by performing this drama, which can be done in a small group or large group setting. The community could then discuss the drama and apply it to their own congregation.

Part 1

CAST:

- Mary, a member of the worship planning committee
- Visitor

SCRIPT:

Mary: Well, hello there. It is so good to welcome you to Faith Church! It's my pleasure to greet you and tell you a bit about our community as we prepare for worship. I've found that a little information can be very helpful. You may have noticed Adam as you came through the door. He is such an amazing singer.

Visitor: Is Adam the person in the wheelchair

Mary: Yes. We don't think it will be for very much longer, but he played his heart out on our church softball team and ended up with a severe knee injury that required surgery. We miss his beautiful tenor voice in the choir.

Visitor: What is that smell? (Covers nose with hand)

Mary: Ah, yes. Edna. Well, she certainly makes her presence known in so many ways. People know she is here before we even see her. Edna is one of our amazing childcare workers. She has held every baby in this church. I know when I picked my children up from nursery, they smelled just like Edna!

Visitor: (Looks around at others in the gathering room).

Mary: I suppose you noticed Ellen. Poor thing! Cancer [said in a whisper]. She is not always able to attend church during her chemotherapy treatment phase [spoken in regular voice]. I've noticed several times when she is absent or heads for the door. Don't be surprised if it happens today. She looks a little green around the gills.

Visitor: Maybe I should head inside church now and get a seat.

Mary: Not before I clue you in to the special surprise. There is a trumpet player in the balcony. I cannot wait for that first song! We will sing and then get ready on that first chorus as he joins us in celebration. People will be so shocked. We didn't even put his name in the bulletin today.

Visitor: Speaking of a bulletin, where can I find the order of worship?

Mary: Oh, yes, I plumb forgot. We decided not to print them anymore. We have always wanted to find a way to redirect some of our budget dollars into making a great website. So, this is the first week we have no order of worship printed.

Visitor: Alright, perhaps now I should head into the worship area.

Mary: Oh my, is that another visitor? With our website being so poor, I wonder how people even find us. It looks like he's not coming past the front door lobby. Checking his phone, looks like. Maybe he got a text from a friend.

Visitor: Could be.

Mary: Well, we will want to get seats soon. Uh-oh. [Mary points toward door]. Looks like Justin is having a rough day. I don't know much about Justin really. I heard he has (in a whisper) autism [said in a whisper]. I know that when he's rocking back and forth like that, it's usually not a good day for him [spoken in a regular voice]. Sometimes his whole family only makes it through a couple of minutes before they have to leave. Well, hard to know how to help. That's for sure. Got to go and grab my seat. I can't wait for that trumpet blast!

(Mary leaves very eager and visitor enters the sanctuary reluctantly).

Part 2

CAST:

- Narrator
- Adam
- Ellen
- Visitor with cell phone
- Justin's mom

SCRIPT:

Narrator: While Mary certainly shared a lot of information as the greeter, it may be helpful to hear from some of the people she mentioned in order to understand their perspectives.

Adam: My name is Adam. I am thankful our church has an elevator. While my use of this wheelchair is most likely temporary, being able to physically access our church has been helpful. Yet it's been hard.

Face it, we don't have a ramp to the choir loft and my voice still works well. I miss singing in the choir. How I wish they had been willing to brainstorm with me to figure out how I could still be part of the choir. The other blow today came right at the beginning of the service. The worship leader said, 'Everybody stand and let's join our voices in praising God together.' Excluded again. How I wish the worship leader had invited us to worship with the phrase 'Please rise in body or in spirit.' Now THAT I could have done. Today I am feeling quite left out.

Ellen: My name is Ellen, and I barely made it out of there in time! Chemotherapy has had lots of interesting effects. One of those is something I've never heard about until this week. Smells are overwhelming to me, and some strong scents can have me running for the bathroom quite quickly. I love Edna, but that perfume is something I can't tolerate right now. Usually, I try to sit in the balcony so I don't smell the perfume, but it was closed off today for some reason. I was seated several rows behind her, but that smell carries a long way! Glad I made it to the parking lot in time. I've heard that some churches have a scent free zone where people who sit in that area agree to come perfume- and cologne-free. That would be so helpful!

Visitor with cellphone: I decided it would be better for me to leave than to enter. I always look things up online before I visit. If it's a new hotel, I can see what's for breakfast, whether to bring my exercise clothes, or what the parking is like. I try to look up restaurants, museums, and even airports. It really helps me know what to expect and brings down my anxiety. So, I was just trying to see if Faith Church had anything online in terms of photos or a video tour. Then I'd be able to see if my clothing fit in or if this is the kind of church where I can raise my hands in worship. I was just uncomfortable going to worship with no advance information. I quickly looked for some kind of order of worship, but there was nothing. I figured it would be better for me to leave than risk the unknown of this community.

Justin's mom: I'm Justin's mom, and this day has not worked out well. Justin usually likes music and enjoys church. He needs a schedule to be comfortable. People might be surprised that he can read words, even though he is unable to speak words. His actions, however, told me something was wrong today. He was waiting by the entrance to church where he always picks up an order of worship. He follows along carefully, even taking that small church pew pencil and checking off each item as we go. I noticed he was rocking when I caught up to him. I found out a little too late that they were no longer printing an order of worship! Did they know how important that is to him? I got him in our regular seat, but then the first hymn started. While he usually loves music, unexpected loud noises are extremely hard for him. We all discovered at the first surprise trumpet blast that Justin can scream more loudly than the trumpet can play. He made it to the car in record time as I chased after him. It took him hours to calm down at home.

Narrator: While these stories happened at Faith Church, what stories have happened in our own communities? How can we create the kind of congregation where Adam, Ellen, the visitor, and Justin's family find a place of welcome and belonging within our congregation?

2: Learn from Others and Share Stories

Show videos such as "Worship as One: Disability in Community" and "One Body," and use the questions designed to spark discussion.[21] Follow blogs and listen to podcasts to immerse yourself in the growing movement that seeks to form inclusive communities that build belonging with people with varied abilities. Explore the ways that a Circle of Congregations has collaboratively created and shared ways they are applying the universal design vision.[22]

3: Utilize Best Practices

I have worked up an online resource page called "Best Practices for Building Belonging in Congregations: Role-Based Tips."[23] The webpage includes a downloadable PDF in both English and Spanish that can help you think about your congregation's universal design plan. Since there are so many links on the page, it would be best to visit the website to explore it fully and find the roles you fill in your congregation.

I'll give you three (the right number, don't you think?) examples of roles to help you better understand the format and value.

Accessibility or Inclusion Advocate or Coordinator

Universal and Responsive Design Tips

1. Identify and recommend changes to overcome barriers for inclusive community.

---

[21] See links on https://allbelong.org/worship-as-one.
[22] Ibid.
[23] Ibid.

2. Coordinate information, training, and other resources to equip your community to include people of all abilities. Your role is to resource existing ministry leaders to include persons with disabilities in their ministries, not house a separate program.
3. Identify and connect with individuals/families impacted by disability to gather information and provide the right support.
4. Along with that individual, advocate for those in your church who have disabilities (for example, offer a discussion with the individual or family to ask the church to make accommodations so they do not have to do it themselves).
5. Equip and support church staff and volunteers; share your appreciation regularly.
6. Learn more about and share All Belong's puzzle piece perspective, theology of inclusion, and the "See/Think/Do" process.

Practical Tools

- See denominational resources such as:
    - Christian Reformed Church and Reformed Church of America's Disability Concerns blog and website for Disability Advocate resources: www.crcna.org/disability
    - United Methodist Church Disability Ministries: https://umcdmc.org
    - Catholic Church Kairos Forum: www.kairosforum.org
    - Presbyterian Church in America, Mission to North America: Engaging Disability with the Gospel, https://pcamna.org/ministry/engaging-disability-with-the-gospel
- Western Theological Seminary offers a graduate certificate in disability and ministry: www.westernsem.edu
- The Christian Leader's Institute has an online course by Barbara Newman and Victoria White on "Creating Congregations of Belonging with People of All Abilities" that

provides a twelve-week overview of this topic.[24] Find out about it at CLI: https://moodle.christianleadersinstitute.org/.
- The *Together* curriculum, created by Friendship Ministries, offers many ideas for adapting inclusive adult small group curriculum to the needs of individuals: https://togethersmallgroups.org.
- Joni and Friends has a short document to help advocates think about how to approach leadership in the church: www.joniandfriends.org/wp-content/uploads/2020/04/talking-to-church-leadership.pdf.
- Dr. Erik Carter's work on the ten dimensions of belonging is a great resource. Watch his presentation on these dimensions: www.youtube.com/watch?v=sRZHwj6CarM.

Preacher

Universal and Responsive Design Tips

1. Know your "big idea" and emphasize this big idea in multisensory ways (for example, make up a catchy phrase, set the big idea to music, show a picture on a PowerPoint slide, have an object to show or interact with, include congregational movement, or make sermon notes with words and pictures).
2. Plant times in the sermon when you encourage interaction between the congregation and the pastor (for example, respond to a question, give a thumbs-up or thumbs-down response, participate in a role play, talk about something with the person next to you, or act out an example or section of Scripture).
3. Think about not only the words you want to say but also how those words will be received. What would you understand if you were an individual with failing memory, a person who interprets language literally, a person with a lower IQ, an

---

[24] "Creating Congregations of Belonging," Christian Leaders Institute, YouTube, December 13, 2019, www.youtube.com/watch?v=NbcBoucRG28.

English language learner, a person with limited hearing, a new believer, or a person from a different country, background, or denomination? How could you change one thing in your sermon to make a better connection?
4. If your sermon is lengthy, consider offering options for movement (for example, a rocking chair for an individual who needs to move, options to sit or stand, a smaller environment where movement is welcome, and hand fidgets or tools available throughout the sanctuary).
5. Watch your wording. "Please rise in body or in spirit" allows all to participate whereas "Please stand" leaves out those who are unable to do so.
6. Consider making a sermon outline available for people to pick up before the service for the sake of people with differences in hearing, attention span, language processing, and memory.
7. Take care when preaching on healing miracles not to assume that all people with disabilities want to be healed.
8. When announcing births of children with disabilities, announce the birth of a child, not a disability.
9. Remember in the congregational prayer people who have nonvisible disabilities, such as asking God for grace for people who have mental health conditions and for their family members.
10. Ask for help! Others in the congregation may be gifted at finding visuals or objects to accompany your ideas, making outlines, or adding in movements.

Practical Tools

- We encourage you to review all of the other roles, including the resources available in each section, to inform your preaching and your support of your congregation.
- View diverse ways of integrating images and universal design elements into your order of worship: www.allbelong.org/church.

- Friendship Ministries offers an inclusive adult Bible study known as *Together*, which has great ideas and techniques that can also apply in a corporate worship setting: https://togethersmallgroups.org.
- Use person-first, honoring language. All Belong offers a Person-First Language Guide from a biblical perspective: www.allbelong.org.
- Visit the Centers for Disease Control and Prevention website for detailed information on disability and inclusion: www.cdc.gov/ncbddd/disabilityandhealth/index.html.
- See the "Person First and Identity First Language" resource on the Employer Assistance and Resource Network on Disability Inclusion (EARN) website: https://askearn.org/page/people-first-language.

Usher

Universal and Responsive Design Tips

1. Receive training on appropriate ways to greet people with disabilities and ask about their needs.
2. Know what your church offers, including gluten-free options, seating options, large-print items, hearing loop, assistants or buddies in children's ministry, quiet area, sound blockers, and more.
3. Be welcoming and understanding of those who do not understand social cues or respond in typical ways.
4. Wear a name tag or other identifiers that signal you are someone to whom guests can come for information or help.
5. If your church doesn't have pew cutouts or flexible chair arrangements, ask that they be created for people who use wheelchairs or walkers.

Practical Tools

- Take a look at sample orders of worship to help you think about how to best support persons with varied abilities worshiping together: see links from www.allbelong.org/worship-as-one.
- The United Methodist Church offers an etiquette and communication guide: https://umcdmc.org/resources/ways-to-welcome-all/etiquette-and-communication.
- Barbara J. Newman's book *Autism and Your Church* has information on understanding individuals who may not recognize social cues in typical ways.
- Use person-first, honoring language. All Belong offers a Person-First Language Guide from a biblical perspective: www.allbelong.org.
- Visit the Centers for Disease Control and Prevention website for detailed information on disability and inclusion: www.cdc.gov/ncbddd/disabilityandhealth/index.html.
- See the "Person First and Identity First Language" resource on the Employer Assistance and Resource Network on Disability Inclusion (EARN) website: https://askearn.org/page/people-first-language.

4: Adult Small Group Curriculum

Are you looking for great adult small group curriculum uniquely designed with the principles of universal design at the forefront? Try the *Together* curriculum in your adult small groups or Sunday school, acknowledging that each group has adults with varied abilities. The options are already built-in! Check out these materials: https://togethersmallgroups.org.

5: Introduce People to Your Church with A Welcome Story

How many of us like to go somewhere that we know nothing about? How much more important might that be for a person with limited mobility, vision, hearing, social skills, or who has anxiety or language or sensory processing differences? A simple tool for introducing your setting is a social story designed to welcome someone into the church, or a *Church Welcome Story*. You can create one for an individual, but you can also create one that is general. It

could be a video, a booklet, or something else. It's a way to preview the space, the people, the expectations, for the viewer/reader to see how they will experience the setting. Many versions and templates can be found online, but here is the start to one as an example.

Part 3
Personalization: Responsive Design

Defining Responsive Design

Responsive Design is the process of getting to know an individual and then responding to that person's strengths and challenges by putting together a personalized plan for use within the activities of the church.

10

Introduction to Personalization: Responsive Design

Let's look once again at the sign by your congregation's door. The

"Everyone Welcome" sign is up, and your community has dismantled many other restriction and exclusion signs through the application of the principles of universal design and universal design for learning. You have created multiple options that are embedded in your church's offerings each week. What could still obscure the welcome sign? Sometimes, even after all that effort, you'll still notice a sign that reads, "Everyone Welcome: Come In. (Andrea, Keesha, Guy, and Harold will still find it difficult to participate.)"

Those names point us to the final part of our three-part plan. While universal design has brought us a long way toward creating community with persons of varied abilities, there will still be some individuals we will want and need to get to know personally and respond to their unique set of strengths and challenges—their greens and pinks. We will need to put together a personalized plan. Responsive design is the process of getting know that person and then responding to the discovered needs (and gifts!) by creating unique avenues of access to the building, programming, or conversation with God in worship.

If creating personalized plans take more time and energy than simply applying universal design alone, why bother? Here are some reasons I think are important.

Scripture. Our congregations are built on the blueprint of what Scripture says about communities. Therefore, the most compelling reason to develop a responsive design plan for specific individuals is clearly found in Scripture. A Scripture-based view of an individual and a God-designed community will be the place you can plant your feet as you make an action plan for your congregation. You will find Scripture-based tools in the "Practical Tools for Bringing Responsive Design to Your Congregation" section.

Personalized plans express commitment to full-puzzle community. This starts with leaders. Because leadership in congregations change, it's important to keep this vision continuously at the forefront. Do all of your pastors and your governing board embrace the vision of building community with people who may need specialized supports to fully participate in your congregation? I have found it can be easy to engage leadership in the principles of universal design for worship due to the big "bang for your buck" and the support it offers to nearly all who are part of the community. But responsive design tests the leaders 'vision of the inestimable worth of each person. When they are willing to say to everybody, "Yes, you belong here; we'll figure out a way to make that work," they do what is needed for that individual, which is the definition of the responsive design vision. Those congregations are excited about the puzzle piece community and are willing to put time, energy, and resources into making sure no one is missing from the puzzle.

Responsive design equips people to minister who may otherwise be overlooked. Individuals who have complex areas of challenge often benefit from a personalized plan for their learning, worship, fellowship, and service in the congregation. John Swinton, in his book *Becoming Friends of Time*, notes the importance of each puzzle piece and the gift each one brings to a community. Where many may struggle to see a person's green areas due to their significant developmental delays, he writes, "It is a vital and most beautiful fact that some members of Jesus' body may simply be called to bear witness to the powerful truth of *being*. In a world that has been seduced by the idolatrous power of speed, clocks, and busyness, bearing witness to the divine significance of simply being is indeed a noble vocation. Being, properly conceived, is a deep and powerful vocation."[25] In what ways can your congregation receive ministry from someone whose calling is to the "ministry of being"? This section will show you a process for putting together plans for individuals (and their families) for situations like these and many others.

Personalized plans can create confidence among all members of the congregation. The person in the center of this plan can be assured that they are well-known, and that equipment and procedures will be in place to promote their safety, communication, and participation. Members of the congregation will be confident in interacting with that individual, having a specific plan to follow whenever necessary. Planning and confidence can be a great antidote for fear and uncertainty—emotions that can get in the way of people worshiping and learning together with people of all abilities.

Some people may need a personalized plan for reasons of safety. The community will need to know how to respond if an individual with a seizure disorder has a seizure while at church. Drinking and eating may be a safety issue when a person needs thickener for any liquid to be consumed safely. The plans do not help everyone in the congregation, because not everyone needs thickener

---

[25] John Swinton, *Becoming Friends of Time: Disability, Timefullness, and Gentle Discipleship* (Waco, TX: Baylor University Press, 2016), 124, italics in original.

or seizure precautions. However, don't be surprised that what you put in place for one individual may show you something that can help many others!

Whatever the situation, it's important to get to know the individual and then respond by putting together a specific plan. In some cases, it will be important to know how an individual communicates needs and wants, with a goal of creating safe ways for an individual to express love for God, make a prayer request, or select a snack from the table. While many of us can use spoken words, others rely on pointing to a picture, using a sign, making a body movement, giving a gesture, or communicating through a digital device.

A person's set of unique areas of gifting and challenge gives the congregation a chance to think deeply and creatively. This is one reason I've seen ministry with persons with varied abilities draw people together across lines that typically divide denominations and faith traditions. Coming together to figure out ways for a beloved individual to best connect with the activities of the church or ways the church can alter a setting to make a better fit for that person unites people.

If you're not eager to read on to find out how to do this, go back to chapter 5 ("Reflections)" in part 1, or go right to the practical tools discussed in chapters 6 and 9 to review ways to engage leadership in thinking about why this matters. When you're ready for it, the next chapter is all about how to apply the responsive design vision.

11

Responsive Design Process

Though responsive design plans will be unique to each individual, I offer here a process you can follow when creating any individualized plan.

Direct the Process

In forming personalized plans, it's important to have a person or committee oversee this process. While a child with a personalized plan can still be under the direction of the children's ministry director or pastor, having an individual with some expertise in forming and supporting that plan will be immensely helpful. Asking that director or coordinator to help an individual transition into the youth department or worship setting will also be helpful. If there is an adult who is experiencing sensory differences due to dementia, the pastor may appreciate an individual who can help plan or set up a team to support that person and the family involved as well as resource the church visitation team with ideas and tools to use for interacting. Personalized plans do not take away from the ownership each ministry leader or pastor has for the individuals who fall under their supervision, but utilizing an expert who can help create, launch, and update plans over time is wise.

In fact, as mentioned in the introduction to this book, this person or committee is integral to the entire three-part plan. This person or committee spreads Puzzle Piece Perspective, sharing the vision of inclusion and equipping leaders with language, training, and resources. Ensuring participation for all, this person or committee is involved in assessing the accessibility of the facility, ministries and spaces, and implementing universal design. Where personalization is needed, this person or committee coordinates the process of personalized planning and oversees launching community teams. Think back to the idea of church ministries being "canned goods," with each "can" representing a different program or committee in the congregation. You will be tempted to think about getting a coordinator who can then own the "can" called disability ministry. While the position of coordinator is vital, the section on participation through universal design reveals that the best people to own this initiative will be those people in charge of each "can," with the coordinator coming alongside the existing leaders. Having a person or a committee that can be a resource for existing staff will be vital in covering the 20-25 percent statistic, as well as the 100 percent vision of universal design. As you look for a coordinator, make sure the job description allows this person to resource others, not own 20-25 percent of the congregation in a "can."

As you look for this coordinator or committee, consider individuals with skills in forming relationships, organizing, equipping people, accessing information and best practices having to do with children and adults with disabilities, and conveying an attitude of shared responsibility. Someone who shows signs of wanting to *own* the individuals involved will not be the best director or coordinator. Someone who refers to individuals with disabilities as "my kids" may well get in the way of others involved in this initiative. Someone who is ready to support, come alongside, and equip others through sharing ideas and responsibilities may be the better fit for this leadership position.

One large congregation found that a committee approach was the best way to connect and support each existing leader. In response to the gamut of needs present in the church—from children to adults—the team consisted of a special educator, an occupational therapist, a parent who provided foster care, a social worker, an individual connected with community resources for adults, and an adult familiar with residential home settings who also has Down syndrome. This team has done a terrific job of coming alongside staff, individuals, and parents as they provide both the "shredded cheese" sprinkle over existing ministries and the necessary expertise to partner with leaders, parents, and individuals in creating and supporting personalized plans.

Define Participants

In many ways, defining the participants in a personalized plan can be a challenging step. Some names may come to mind immediately. In other cases, parents of a child or an adult with a disability may not see the need for a plan.

In general, I can envision four scenarios as we go about finding out who may best be supported with a responsive design plan.

In one scenario, you can tell at a glance. An individual who is a wheelchair user and unable to communicate with words finds it difficult to get into the church worship area. It's clear from just one glance that a plan needs to be in place. The accessibility coordinator or committee can quickly spring into action.

The next scenario is one in which an individual speaks to leadership and lets them know that they or someone they know will need a plan. A parent expresses to the children's ministry leader that her child has been diagnosed with autism and will need some support to be included on Wednesday nights. An adult writes on the welcome tablet that he lives with significant anxiety and will need some support to attend worship and other church events. The church knows that a plan is needed because someone has raised a situation or concern. Again, this awareness provides a simple opportunity for the coordinator to spring into action with a plan.

The third scenario involves the perspective of others, which means it isn't always easy to know how to proceed. One of the church's Sunday school classes has been staffed with two extra volunteers for four years because of the intensity of the participants' needs—one specific child in particular. A ministry group leader has an adult in their group who has no idea how many prayer requests are appropriate in one group meeting, or someone else in the group is being shunned because of that person's differences in social skills. The Sunday school teacher and the ministry group leader see a person who could benefit from a responsive design plan, but the parent or the individual may not be aware of this issue. It's possible, especially in the case of children, that parents choose not to disclose differences because of bad experiences, differing cultural perspectives, or the fear of being singled out. Once they see how you handle other situations with love and support, they may step forward later.

While it's wise to think about some universal design features to add to this environment and to pray about an opening for further conversation, I also highly recommend the "I Notice" conversation in chapter 15 ("Practical Tools for Bringing Responsive Design to Your Congregation") for help in how to respond to these situations.

Finally, the fourth scenario is one in which you have individuals who may benefit from a personalized plan, but you aren't given much information about them due to legal protections. Even though you may want to put a plan in place, care providers can't give you the information you need because they have to follow confidentiality rules for paid caregivers of persons with disabilities.

My suggestion is to begin with those who would like a plan. Here are a few ways they can let you know:

- Provide the name and contact information of the right person to connect with to request accommodations or support—for example, your accessibility advocate, the person in charge of an event or ministry, or someone in the office who can get the ball rolling.

- Especially in children and youth programming, include some key questions on the general registration form that will allow all parents to provide information about their child's green strengths and pink struggles.
- Distribute congregational surveys with questions related to support or accommodations in order to identify who may be on the fringes or staying home because of fear that their needs will not be met.
- Equip leaders to look for and listen to individuals who may benefit from a personalized plan, teaching these leaders how to observe and express their observations in an "I Notice" kind of conversation.

Sometimes it's clear that a plan is needed, but it seems to be a difficult or awkward topic to bring up with parents. Perhaps they did not indicate some of the issues you are noticing. Perhaps they are unaware of some developmental differences because this is their oldest child. Perhaps church is the child's first social setting, and it's a hard adjustment. In that case, it may be important to learn how to have the "I Notice" conversation with parents as you consider a personalized plan to support that child. It's also possible to use this conversation in the context of speaking with an adult who may benefit from a personalized plan.

Remember that a person's needs change over time. A child with autism spectrum disorder who was covered well under the universal design features in the children's ministry may benefit from a responsive design plan as they head into youth group. An adult who has served on church council, led Bible studies, and been a member of the church for many years may begin to show signs of dementia or experience a stroke. Now this individual may need the support of a personalized plan. Be aware that some will only temporarily need this type of personalized support.

Make sure you let each participant know you will enter into a process to really get to know them, and, along with that person, you will put together a plan so that the church setting will provide a better fit. Make sure you let that person know the plan is just as much for the individual as it is for the church as a whole. The plan will allow the congregation to support or better include that person, who will surely be used by God to reach and touch this congregation with their gifts and presence. A responsive design plan benefits everyone in the community.

To respond to a person's unique, God-designed knitting pattern, you have the privilege of discovering the greens and pinks that make up this person's life. It is important to find out what is easy and what is difficult for this individual. How would this person like to serve in the church? What programs or offerings would this person like to be part of? It would be helpful to know how this person takes in and processes information and how this person communicates and expresses needs, thoughts, and ideas to others. You can use a printed form (or an online form) to gather this information in writing, or the questions may better be asked in an interview. This is one of the forms I highly encourage you to personalize each time you use it. As you think about the individual, add, and delete questions based on what you already know. We have created a basic form template[26] intended for you to personalize for each specific situation.

Design the Plan

You will want to make this plan in conjunction with the individual and/or the parent or guardian. Depending on the individual, this plan may primarily focus on the worship setting. Another person may have a plan that encompasses other programs offered by the church.

---

[26]See links at https://allbelong.org/worship-as-one.

Because of the many possibilities, I recommend thinking in four distinct areas or quadrants.

The four quadrants represent four areas in which churches typically provide for any individual in that community. A church usually offers opportunities for *worship, education, fellowship,* and *service*. While you may end up adding another area based on congregation's unique makeup, these are four key areas to consider. For example, if you discover that an adult has a significant gluten allergy but doesn't have spoken words with which to voice that allergy or reject certain foods, this issue may impact the celebration of the Lord's Supper, but it may also be important to form a plan in the fellowship or education areas where that person will be present. Note, too, that another individual in that situation may desire only to participate in worship, so the personalized form will contain only that information for that setting.

The other crucial feature of this planning process is the recognition that there must be two parts to any area of the plan. *Every good plan has two parts!* The plan is for the individual, and the plan is for "the others." Yes, we need to be focused on the individual, but we also need to consider the resources, learning opportunities, or information that the peers or volunteers need in order to make this plan succeed. For example, you may discover that a child who is highly sensitive to unexpected noises may scream and cover both ears when the noise happens. Your plan for the individual will likely include making sure noise-cancelling headphones are available, as well as telling parents in advance when the youth praise band will be leading worship. That is part of the plan for the individual.

The others, however, in this situation are the peers, who may need information about how God makes people whose ears are different. A noise that may be loud to someone may not be loud to someone else. They will better understand their peer if they know about this hearing sensitivity. Also, those who run the sound system will benefit from information about appropriate decibel levels in any setting where this person is present.

Even more important than the details of the plan will be the people you gather together. Make sure, first of all, that the individual is present and in control of this plan to the fullest extent possible. Then gather people who support, love, and know this individual. Knowing the equipment and procedures that must be in place for safety and participation will also be important. Use the puzzle piece community in helping to form the plan[27].

Draw Together Resources

Most plans require people, equipment or supplies, and education or training. It's important to gather who and what you need for making your plan work. If, for example, your plan says you'll have a space where this person can take a break, you will need to create such a space. If your plan states that you're going to have an adult buddy in a youth group setting with an individual, you will need to recruit a person or team for that role. All communities vie for the attention of volunteers, and it's easier for people to volunteer once they know exactly what you need. For example, it's one thing to say, "We need some helpers with Braydon"; it's another thing to say, "We're looking for two people to partner with Braydon during Sunday night youth group twice a month." Being specific will help people decide if they can participate.

In addition, make sure you take time to complete the necessary training for implementing your plan. It's exciting when you have the people resources lined up, but people who have the necessary information and training for completing their part of the plan will always be your *best* volunteers. You know your training is complete

---

[27] See https://allbelong.org/worship-as-one for a Responsive Design Plan Template

when you can look each team member in the eye and hear their enthusiastic response when you ask, "Do you have what you need to participate in this plan?" Knowing about the person will help volunteers. See chapter 15 for more about getting to know and sharing about an individual with a quick reference I call a *Getting to Know Me Sheet*.

Distribute the Plan (with permission!)

In most cases, multiple people will be involved in a personalized plan. For example, if an individual needs an adaptation in order to participate in the Lord's Supper, the people who serve the elements will need that information—which can involve several people. Therefore, it's helpful to put both the plan and any significant and honoring information about an individual in a format that allows you to share it with those in the congregation who have a need to know. Before you can share information about a specific individual, however, you must have permission. *Make sure you have obtained proper permission* before sharing with anyone beyond the coordinator or the person gathering the information and helping to form the personalized plan. The plan template includes a section for gaining permission to share information.

Once you have interviewed the individual and parent or guardian and set up a personalized plan, consider putting that information in a one-page snapshot to give to others once the written permission form is in place. Many variations are possible, depending on the person involved.

Here are some ideas on personalized plans from congregations I've worked with:

- For a child who attended Sunday school and the Wednesday night boy's club, the leaders of those groups needed a quick snapshot of that child and the personalized plan. Those leading

the music and games times also needed that information. The accessibility coordinator designed a cover sheet similar to the sample above and then attached the personalized plan to that sheet to hand out to the leaders.
- There is no need to limit yourself to paper options. An adult was eager to share his puzzle piece with the church community, so they used a video format to interview that person. The video was shown to the entire community as part of a worship service where the inclusion plan was briefly laid out. The information was also written down for use now and in the future.
- Another adult loved baseball. The congregation had information printed up like baseball cards so this individual could distribute them to people in his social environments. It was a great tool for all involved.

Debrief

After the plan is up and running, take time to check on everyone involved. Some congregations gather the team that surrounds a person and celebrate what has gone well and brainstorm ways to strengthen the plan. Since people change over time, make sure you review the plan when anything major changes for the individual (or at least once a year).

I have known many congregations that see the benefit of having personalized plans, and I have discovered two unique factors important to mention in connection with these plans: (1) cultural perspectives (addressed in the next chapter) and (2) situations in which an individual or family presents an opportunity for the congregation to engage in a more encompassing way that goes beyond participation in church-specific activities (addressed in chapter 13).

12

Cultural Considerations for Personalized Plans

It's crucial to bear in mind the cultural differences that can come into play when personalized plans are created. In my work with All Belong, I've had the opportunity to partner with individuals who have researched some of the views related to persons with disabilities in other countries and cultures. A great variation in understanding, emotion, and response exists. It's important to note, for example, that one culture may view even just the word *disability* with a great deal of shame or embarrassment. In some cultures, a person may expect the church family to offer many supports and therefore be highly active in their lives, given their cultural understanding of the church as family. Understanding that cultural perspective will be important to research and understand before approaching that individual or family.

When speaking to a group in the Seattle area in October 2018, Dr. María Cornou noted that it's important to understand how individuals in that culture view the "cause" of disability, as well as to understand the family roles within that culture. For some cultures, the perspective is that disability involves a "sin issue" and therefore may link disability to the word *shame* or embarrassment.[28] In her research with congregations from many different countries, she found that some prefer to hide the fact that they have a family member with a disability. In addition, family values may also play a role. For example, in one culture it may be the expectation of the mother to care for the children.

---

[28] See María Cornou, "Universal Design for Worship: Consider Cultural Differences," shared at an event (Renovate Church: Creating a Space for All Abilities) in Bothell, Washington, October 24, 2018.

This is her job and how well she does it equates to her own value and worth. If a church approached this parent and suggested she would benefit from some help, it may come across as an insult as opposed to a blessing to the family.

In her presentation, Dr. Cornou noted that it's important to first develop trust on the part of the family members involved and then do research to gain more understanding about that particular cultural view of both the word *disability* and the family roles. She also says that "worshiping together can help people from different cultures mutually experience each other's gifts, extend reciprocal hospitality, learn from each other and model Christian fellowship."[29] This clearly echoes the idea of inclusion but reminds us also to intentionally give and receive information and extend welcome, without assumptions, as we all seek a common goal—namely, to glorify God.

Reverend Dr. LaTonya Penny has done her doctoral research in thinking about disability in the African American church. She notes that the experience of slavery brought about a strong perspective that is crucial to understand. If a parent gave birth to a child with a disability, there was a good chance they would try to hide that child and the disability from the slaveholders. It may have been the child's only chance for survival. Both the history of slavery and the tradition of hospitality are true, and both are part of the story when thinking about worshiping with persons with disabilities who are part of the African American tradition.

I am thankful for the ongoing research from both Dr. Cornou and the Rev. Dr. Penny and look to them for ongoing leadership and ideas in this area. Many of us belong to multicultural congregations, and we

---

[29] "María Eugenia Cornou on the Myth of Hispanic Culture," Calvin Institute of Christian Worship, November 3, 2015, https://worship.calvin.edu/resources/resource-library/maria-eugenia-cornou-on-the-myth-of-hispanic-culture.

need additional tools and better avenues for mutual understanding. In an effort to learn from others around the world, as well as to share ideas like those presented in this book with ministry leaders in training, All Belong partnered with the Christian Leaders Institute to create a course that is now available online. Participants in the course reflect on their own community's culture and attitudes toward disability.[30]

We continue to learn more about how culture informs belief about curses, sin, shame, as well as perceptions of divine or spiritual connection to or through a disability (not to mention the differences in what is considered a disability), all impact a community's understanding of and interactions with people with disabilities. It is also clear, however, that God is at work around the planet uniting Christ's body, drawing together members of all abilities as active participants in God's kingdom. We must listen carefully and intentionally to others as we plan with them for their full participation in the life of the church.

---

[30] For more information, visit the Christian Leaders Institute website: www.christianleadersinstitute.org.

13

Becoming Community Using Teams

By Victoria White

In some cases, persons with disabilities have access to support through insurance plans or have community mental health supports. Some individuals have families that consider it their duty and are eager to come alongside that person. Yet the reality is that these supports are not available to some, or for others these supports are simply not enough. As you learn about the situations of individuals in the responsive design process, you may find that their need for support is significant. Crises or significant needs for support may have been what drew a person or family to the church in the first place. This is when a community team can come alongside an individual or family at church and help them find ways to participate fully—in short, they will essentially *be* church for them. This will mean developing interdependence, which is a beautiful way of building community.

This idea is not new. Leaders in the field of disability and faith have noted over the years the need for intentional support. Stephanie Hubach informs on the situation for churches and families as she describes what she calls care groups:

Curiosity and genuine concern on the part of the church members can feel overwhelming to a family when it comes in the form of countless requests for information. The care group provides the family with a sense of privacy and normalcy by serving as a conduit for appropriate and relevant information . . . The care group mobilizes the congregation to provide emotional, physical, and spiritual support. By channeling the congregation's offers of assistance in concrete and organized ways, the care group allows the family to feel the caring presence of the church through effective ministry.[31]

Collaborators in faith and disability initiatives produced a short resource on supportive care in the congregation and noted that this care is expressed in "a circle of persons who desire to experience the potential of mutual growth that comes from serving one another."[32] Lamar Hardwick, a man known as the "autism pastor" who urges the Christian community to think more intentionally about persons with disabilities, mentions a "care plan . . . to meet the family's spiritual needs, deploying the resources required. 'Even though our outer nature is wasting away, our inner nature is being renewed day by day' (2 Corinthians 4:16)."[33]

Following Hardwick's lead, let's look to Scripture for a way to think about what we will define as "community teams." Catch a glimpse at the way the early church handled the needs of its members: "All the believers were one in heart and mind . . . They shared everything they had . . . God's grace was so powerfully at work in them all that there were no needy persons among them . . . [All] was distributed to anyone who had need" (Acts 4:32–35).

The puzzle piece perspective has taught us the value of each person in our communities. Not only is each person worthy of our doing whatever it takes to welcome them as those who truly belong in our community, but maybe—just maybe—entire congregations will come alive ("one in heart and mind," with "God's grace so powerfully

---

[31] Stephanie O. Hubach, *Same Lake, Different Boat: Coming Alongside People Touched by Disability* (2006; repr., Phillipsburg, NJ: P&R, 2006),192–93.
[32] Dean Preheim-Bartel et al., *Supportive Care in the Congregation* (Goshen, IN: Mennonite Publishing, 2011), 48.
[33] Lamar Hardwick, *Disability and the Church: A Vision for Diversity and Inclusion* (Downers Grove, IL: InterVarsity, 2021), 140.

at work") through the interactions that are happening as a result of meeting the needs of individuals and families.

Not every responsive design plan will include this kind of involvement, but do consider this option for situations in which the church can support an individual or family in a deeper, more intense way, committing to the kind of creativity it can take for that person or family to contribute to the community in ways that are tailored to their needs and gifts.

There are a variety of ways community teams can support families or individuals, ranging from support that takes place primarily in the church or worship setting to a far more encompassing support of the individual's or family's life.

On one end of this spectrum are the "at church" teams. Years ago, when All Belong was known as CLC Network, it adapted the strategy used in school settings of "wraparound support teams" and playfully nicknamed them "G.L.U.E. teams"—people who stuck together as those **G**iving, **L**oving, **U**nderstanding, and **E**ncouraging the individual and/or family in the church setting. The process for forming the teams was laid out in the *G.L.U.E. Training Manual* and has introduced hundreds of churches to a way of supporting individuals who require a responsive design plan for their time in a worship setting and in the church community.[34]

On the other end of the spectrum are the "being the church" teams. I have been the recipient of this type of intentional, life-encompassing support. Several years ago, Lyme disease invaded my neurological system, and I found myself unable to attend church. The energy expended to get across the large, open spaces of the parking lot into a crowded and noisy entryway; the rush of sound waves

---

[34] Barbara J. Newman and Kimberly Luurtsema, *G.L.U.E. Training Manual* (Wyoming, MI: CLC Network, 2009)

battering my every receptor; the anxiety of interacting with multiple people, each with their movements and sounds—all of this was more than my body and brain could handle. I actually ended up in an emergency room due to hyperventilation and seizure-like convulsions a couple of times trying to do it.

Add to this several other complicating factors, such as the kids' sensory differences, multiple family members with diagnosed anxiety, and then my husband's neck surgery, it became clear we weren't going anywhere for a few months without help. We needed a team that would wrap itself around our lives. A friend began a care team for us based on a model from the book titled *Share the Care*.[35] The team took on the responsibility of ensuring that our family not only had opportunities to worship and experience fellowship but also had meals and groceries, clean laundry, transportation to appointments, and much more.

The spectrum of Community Teams: community engagement for support:

- DURING church
- AROUND church (before, after, etc.)
- EXTENDING INTO other areas of LIFE

The process recommended here comes from both personal and professional experiences and draws on the legacy of resources such as the ones quoted at the beginning of this chapter. It may seem daunting to think of supporting even one individual during the few hours a week at church, let alone an entire family's needs on an ongoing basis. However, whether for "at or around church" or extending further into

---

[35] Cappy Capossela and Sheila Warnock, *Share the Care: How to Organize a Group to Care for Someone Who Is Seriously Ill* (New York: Fireside, 2004).

everyday life, here's a simple ready-set-go system for engaging the community, followed by examples.

Becoming Support: Ready? Ask Questions.

Ask: Would you like a community team? As we noted in chapter 12, how a family or individual responds to the church's efforts can vary. Start with listening to what the individual and/or family are open to. Emphasize your desire that they contribute to the community, as well as your joy at coming alongside them in their situation.

Ask: What can the team do? If you discovered significant needs in the responsive design process, you may want to gather specifics about these needs so you can form a community team. These are the kinds of questions you could ask: Would this family like a few meals? How often? Are there dietary restrictions? Do they need rides? When? For how many people? At this point, you may also want to pass the baton of leadership for this team to a team leader. More information about this role and the role of other team members is at the end of this chapter.

Ask: Who would you like on the team? The more life-encompassing the supports will be, the more important it will be to involve family and close friends, even if they are not part of your congregation. Team members can include buddies during church—possibly from the children's ministry area or a mentorship ministry already in place in the church. If meals are needed, you can draw on the hospitality ministry that sets schedules to bring meals to people who've just had a baby or have undergone surgery. If transportation is an issue, you may have people who bring a vanload or busload of people to church regularly and can add this family as well.

The community team has a central focus on one individual or family as compared to ministries that carry out a particular responsibility, regardless of who it is for. The greater the list of needs, the longer the list of potential team members will be. Outside of your congregation, you may add to the team Cub Scout leaders, teachers, bus drivers, coworkers, or others—depending on the situation of the family or individual. Imagine the possibilities for God's kingdom to spread as you wrap your arms around a family and as people in their lives begin to interact with you!

The team may exist for a brief time or for years. The team will undoubtedly change over time as needs change and as team members move on to other commitments—and that's okay! By having this intentional structure, people can come on and go off the team as needed while the necessary supports are maintained. That structure also provides ways for relationships to form and grow, as well as for the individual or family at the center of it to explore how they can contribute to the life of the congregation as they get to know the people on their team.

To form an effective team, it's important to know some things about each team member. This is where the puzzle piece perspective becomes extremely practical, and where a good system for housing the information becomes essential. Each team member has strengths, availabilities, and skills that may fit the needs of the family or individual in a particular way.

1. What do you love to do, and what would you enjoy doing for this family or person?
2. What would you rather not do?

It's important to give people permission, to even encourage them to say yes to only the things they're willing to do, and no to the things they're not willing to do. Again, the greater the amount of needs to meet, the greater the size of the team so no one will feel trapped, overwhelmed, burnt-out, or overburdened.

Team members should be expected to share their contact information and preferences. This information can be housed in such a way that other team members and the family or individual can access it, such as in a shared online document or through everyone using an app such as ianacare, which is a family caregiving support tool.

My team used Google Sheets as a shared database (Workbook) that contained a page (spreadsheet) of names, addresses, phone numbers, emails, and so forth. Another sheet contained the availability and expressed preferences of each team member, sometimes with an accompanying note that the person lived far away but was willing to pray or provide funding, or that the person had limitations or required accommodations in order to participate.

Think of the structure of support as coming around the individual or family:

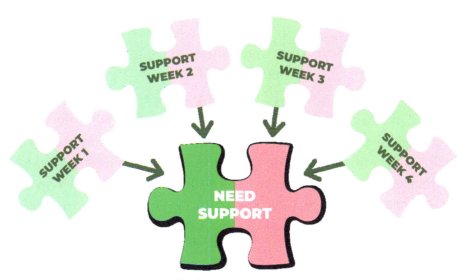

Becoming support: Set?

Set up communication that works for the team. Communication is crucial for its success. Therefore, the team leader should begin with the gathered information and share stated needs from the family or individual with the team members. This is done best in person so everyone can discuss the needs. The family or individual needs to know who is on the team, along with their roles, contact information, preferences, and availability. Once this has been established, everyone will know how best to contact one another.

Sharing some information with the congregation is important as well so that everyone can surround the family and the team in prayer. Any information shared with the congregation must be done with permission from the individual or family with regard to their situation and needs. The information can be given through the church prayer list, a Facebook page or group, bulletin, newsletter, Twitter, or email list, or can be communicated from the pulpit. This is the opportunity for your congregation to be "one in heart and mind."

Set the pieces in place. Are you ready for the fun part? Putting the puzzle together is exciting! After the team leader publishes a list of needs, you will see how the community comes together. Kids learn to serve by playing with young children whose parent needs a break, or by helping bake muffins and bringing them to the family. How much more fun it is for people to do daily errands when they do them together, taking someone who can't drive to the grocery store and eye doctor. Watch relationships bloom as mentors spend time with young people who struggle with social interactions in a large busy church setting but who really desire to grow in the Lord and learn how to participate in corporate worship, fellowship, education, and service.

The possibilities are as plentiful as the reasons and the ways in which these teams form. My team leader was deeply blessed and encouraged by the responses she got from team members after seeing our immense list of needs. Like many families you will encounter, our family was surrounded by people who knew of my difficult situation but had no idea how to help. This process gave them a clear and organized way to help someone they cared about and gave specific ways to stay connected to my family, as we were finding ourselves increasingly isolated by our situation. It provided fresh life to friendships, brought "off-duty" missionaries back into a place of ministering with their gifts (greens), and gave everyone a sense of belonging.

As the pinks and greens form the puzzle, it will become clear what is working and what is not. Some team members may be better at punctuality than others. Some have more reliable transportation than others. Some are great at doing laundry the "right way" for the family. Some have a knack for shopping someone's grocery list, and some are happy to take a person with them to run errands. Some are really good at helping an agitated individual calm down and express why they're distressed.

Any number of factors may need adjustment. Life is messy. The more lives involved and the longer the span of time, the messier it can get. So, the team must be flexible—as must the family that is receiving the support. Regular check-ins with team members and open lines of communication about the functioning of the team are vital to the team's survival and success. Everyone must agree to acknowledge when something isn't a perfect fit and allow another puzzle piece to try to fill that spot as we serve together in God's grace.

Set the tone: celebrate. Every group of people united for a purpose needs to take time to celebrate together. This allows the group to bond, relate, relax, and refresh. And of course, food helps! Especially for a group that has continued on for many years, a regular gathering at least once a year is necessary and enjoyable. A new group should gather once initially to meet one another. It is quite likely that many of the team members don't know one another, and some may not even know the family or individual well. They should gather again in no less than six months to celebrate what is working well and to discuss necessary changes; new ways of sharing information; brainstorming ideas for the group; whether to add, subtract, or replace team members, evaluate needs on the list, or talk about any other details. When a team is no longer needed, it can be an absolute delight to have a closing celebration as well.

Set the tone: look for the grace to both give and receive help. Some people are better at asking for and receiving help than others. Some people are way too good at it. A community team puts structure to the needs that have been identified by at least one person outside of the immediate situation and that can be met by a variety of people. The family or individual around whom you wrap your arms may need a bit of coaching in what is appropriate to ask for or in how to be gracious receivers.

Set the tone: flexibility is key. I learned firsthand that the family or individual receiving support will also have to understand that "everything is optional," meaning that all needs and plans are subject to going unmet or being changed. Appointments sometimes had to be changed because no one was available for transportation at the scheduled time, for example. People get sick sometimes. Team members have family situations arise. Each person on the team has their own life and their own needs as well. Everyone must agree from the beginning, and be reminded often, that the point of this community team is to provide support and a sense of community, and the flawless following of an original plan or schedule is not at all the point. When in a church service setting, a more consistent set of support can be expected than when the team is wrapping around a family's life in a greater way, but the principle of understanding and flexibility still applies.

Set the tone: participate in *joy*. Supporting an individual or family is not something you sign up to do because it is your job. You could be doing it out of a sense of guilt or duty but be aware that this motivation generally doesn't lead to good outcomes. This endeavor is characterized by ministry, by the acts of service.

But that doesn't mean it's all "me serving you"—team members providing support for the individual or family. In fact, the best-functioning and most long-lasting teams work well because of the ministry that happens *both ways*. The individual or family minister to their team members in their expressions of gratitude, in the grace they display in willingly receiving the meals that didn't come out perfectly, the groceries that were a little different than what they expected, or the helpful ideas that ended up being not so helpful. They can pray for their team members, leaders, and coordinator. They can tell the story of their community team to their congregation and to others, showing off how God's people are doing God's work—how they are being the church! And there are hundreds of other ways that the individual's or family's unique "greens" can be used in the interdependent community this team facilitates.

See the Community Team as Interdependent:

Set the tone: caregivers need support. Caregivers, whether paid full-time workers, parents, children, spouses, or other family members, are often the lone support for an individual—sometimes even for several individuals. A community team does not replace a caregiver. In fact, it may be that the caregiver is the one who needs support more! Quite often a team is seen as necessary when the church notices an overwhelmed caregiver. Support is meant not to replace a caregiver but to come alongside and encourage them. Consider a support group for caregivers if you have several in the congregation or your community has opportunities to interact often with those in a caregiver role.

Becoming Support: Go!

The practical dimensions of how a team works follows a simple structure, as pictured in the graphics in this chapter. While there will be differences in every community and situation, four main points of contact generally work well, with one coordinator or team leader overseeing the team (who may or may not be one of the four points of contact or who can serve as a "fifth week" and sub when needed).

I think of the roles within these teams as specific parts of the body—the body of Christ!

Roles of a Community Team

Your community and the individual or family you are coming alongside will ultimately define how these roles look, but here are some guidelines to get you on your way to defining the roles on a community team.

The Individual or family the Team forms around: The Heart

This person or family is an active participant in a successful team.

Tasks:

- Communicate needs
- Receive support with grace
- Contribute to the lives of team members and the church

Team Leader: The Central Nervous System

When the team is for in-church and around-church support, this person may be a staff member (care pastor or coordinator, inclusion, or accessibility director) or be a member of the ministry teams. Setting up teams will be a natural part of responsive design planning for individuals where one-on-one assistance or other in-depth support is needed for individuals to fully participate as co-laborers in Christ during church events. When the team is for the-rest-of-life situations, this person may be on staff or part of the church, or they may be a family friend who knows and cares deeply about what is going on and is able to connect people from inside as well as outside the weekend-gathering church community.

Tasks:

- Gather information from prospective team members and from the family or individual
- Set up a place to hold and share the information within the group.
- Filter team members' information to identify the best fit for each member.
- Host an introductory gathering to kick-off the team and share the vision for this micro community.
- Thank team members for their parts in wrapping around and supporting (verbalizing it before they leave the church that day, sending a quick text or email when you know they were at the family's home, or dropping a note in the mail regularly).

- Check on how the team is functioning, adjust details as needed, and hold celebration gatherings at various times to keep the team enjoying one another and serving one another well.

Team Members: The Hands & Feet of the Team

In-church and around-church team members are the people who will be the one-on-one buddies in the worship service or the person who goes to the house before the family arrives at church to help with getting ready, transition support, rides, or other identified needs.

When teams are supporting the-rest-of-life, and the team is supporting multiple areas of life, it is helpful to establish what could be thought of as team organizers. It may be divided among four people, each taking the role for one or two weeks at a time.

Tasks

- Find out what the needs are for the week/two weeks/month.
- Contact other team members to help meet as many of the needs as possible. One of the greatest gifts to an individual or family is setting them free from always having to be the ones asking for help from friends, family, and others. It also takes away from the volunteers the pressure of answering the family directly.
- Handle any emergency calls from the individual or family during your designated time period.
- Verify that other team members are completing what they agreed to do, and navigate changes to the plan (for example, the times when team members aren't able to complete a task they agreed to do)

Expectations:

- Give contact and preference information to the team leader and update it when something changes.
- Be flexible.
- Be willing to learn about the area of illness, disability, or difference that affects the individual or family you are supporting, which may involve getting some training.
- Offer to use your skills and areas of green.
- Be honest about your level of commitment and your own boundaries.
- Take care of yourself and your own family, which sometimes means saying no to requests from the weekly organizer.
- Look for ministry moments and relationship-building opportunities through your role on the team.

Team members are the ones who will receive ministry *from* the individual or family the most often, and they will see and experience the most direct contact with the nitty-gritty of life with a disability or area of need. In the next chapter, you'll find a few examples of these teams at work.

14
Learning from Congregations using Responsive Design

To honor confidentiality with regard to individuals and their specific situations, I will list three examples from congregations in North America but will not supply real names or locations. I know these people and congregations well. The examples will cover features of a responsive design plan for both children and adults. As you read, notice:

- How each story coordinates with one or more steps of the personalized responsive design plan.
- How the person with the disability is included in making the plan. There's an insightful phrase that is appropriate to remember here: "Nothing about us without us." It's important, whenever possible, to include the individual in the process
- That every good plan has two parts—one part for the individual and one part for providing information, resources, and supports for peers, congregation members, volunteers, and leaders.

1. David's Responsive Design Plan

The youth group leaders were becoming nervous. David was about to enter youth group. The children's ministry leader was also nervous about sending David to the next level of programming. David, a fifth grader with autism spectrum disorder, had done very well in the children's program, but seemed to be irritating his peers recently. He would get too close to their faces and the boys in particular were becoming less tolerant of this behavior. They were backing away from him and starting to make jokes *about* him, not *with* him.

David seemed oblivious to this, but the leaders knew something needed to be done. They asked the accessibility coordinator to help them put together a plan. She got to know David, who had an amazing gift for memorization and loved technology. By spending time watching David and talking with him and his parents, she also discovered that he really did want to have friends at church but didn't always use the best techniques in getting peers to enter into that friendship with him.

The coordinator gathered David, his parents, his current Sunday school teacher, the youth group leader, and a trusted family friend and put together an inclusion plan. The plan had two parts—it focused mainly on the youth group (education) and worship settings, and also had some portions that addressed David's individual needs. David was eager to use his gifts in God's service, so he would be joining the technology team to help during the worship service, and the youth pastor agree to talk to the senior pastor and suggest that David use his gifts of memorization by reciting the Scripture of the day from time to time from the pulpit.

The youth group leaders were eager to learn more about autism spectrum disorder, as well as dig into specific insights into David's God-designed puzzle piece, so they asked a church consultant from All Belong to do a presentation on ASD as part of an adult education session and a separate session for the youth group leaders. David and his peers would be doing the puzzle piece lesson together with the current Sunday school teacher, but the youth group pastor would be present during this time. David's current teacher would use that lesson to not only highlight the puzzle pieces of several children in her group, but especially to introduce David's greens and pinks to the group. She and the youth group leader would emphasize the community aspect of the puzzle piece design and address the group members about the difference between "laughing *at*" and "laughing *with*." Parents and the trusted friend committed to interact with David's school to produce a plan that would teach David correct social distance. They would then bring those ideas to his leaders at church.

David's plan was reviewed at the end of his first year in youth group, and things were going very well. Everyone learned and grew from this time of focused attention on ASD and on David. Because the leaders felt equipped, the peers had the information they needed and were getting along well, and little turnover took place in the youth group leadership for the next years. David's individual plan lasted for only one year. The coordinator agreed to check up on David every once in a while, just to make sure everything was going well.

2. The Miller Family's Community Team

The congregation was surprised to find out the Millers had another child at home. Family members took turns staying home with Jordan or occasionally hired someone to come in. Given Jordan's love for music and the parents' desire to raise each child in the church, they were hoping at some point that he could attend. They were also aware that his bedroom walls were full of holes. He had command of just a few words, so punching and kicking were ways he would communicate when frustrated. The family couldn't imagine that church would be a great place for Jordan due to his aggressive responses.

When a member of the congregation, however, found out that the Millers had another child who had never been to church, they asked the accessibility coordinator to begin forming a plan. Several individuals in the church already had responsive design plans, so this was a familiar process in the church. After learning more about Jordan, the coordinator knew it was time to suggest a community team. This congregation did not have any of these teams up and running, but Jordan's presence at church was going to be challenging, and the level of fatigue of the parents and siblings was overwhelming.

They had no relatives close by, and they had been members of this church for a year. It was high time.

With the family's permission, the coordinator explained the situation to the pastor. The pastor intentionally set out to get to know Jordan and his unique puzzle piece. The team built an initial plan and summarized it to the congregation during a morning worship service so they could also announce the need for volunteers.

The pastor said, "I am delighted to introduce you to another member of the Miller family—Jordan. He has a love for music, and that music makes him move and dance. We are going to give Jordan access to the ramp area during worship on Sundays so that he can move as we worship. I have noticed God has not freed many of us to move during worship, and I'm eager to have Jordan serve as a role model during worship. Also, we're having a meeting after church this morning for about thirty minutes. We know that Jordan's presence at church and our support for his family during the week provide an amazing new opportunity for us. We will be looking for four volunteers to serve as team leaders, as well as several volunteers to be team members with Jordan for some parts of the worship service. We will be looking for someone who may be able to prepare materials we can use with Jordan to teach him more about Jesus. We'd also love to find some people who will support the family on Wednesdays with a meal brought to the home, since they are busy with therapy sessions on that day. We know other needs may arise from time to time with transportation and support for Jordan's siblings. Come find out more about Jordan and how you might be able to join the Miller family's community team. We will give you all the information you need to see if this can work for you. I would like to see at least twenty-five of us show up for this meeting today. My wife and I and our two teens will be there, and we've already committed to being a part of the Miller family's community team."

It was a wonderful place to begin. While a particularly rough day came when Jordan introduced one of the church walls to his favorite decorative hole, the team was prepared in advance and knew just how to respond. Jordan now not only attends worship, but he has also joined the youth group with members of his community team who are also part of the youth group. Jordan's peers are quick to pick him up for football games or other events. The Millers now have an email group at the ready should they need support or help. This community team has had a few members go on and off given a variety of circumstances, but membership has been remarkably stable, with each person offering support when the list of needs is presented by the week's organizer (team leader) on Mondays.

3. Gloria's Responsive Design Plan and Community Team

The pastor was the one person in the congregation who knew Gloria. Gloria's family lived close by, but they found it hard to talk about their adult daughter who lives with bipolar disorder. When Gloria remembered to take her medications, life went more smoothly than on the days she did not remember. The pastor often saw Gloria during the week as she paced in the parking lot of the church. She would join her at times, offering a cup of coffee and conversation as they walked back and forth together. It became clear, however, that the pastor was the only one comfortable interacting with Gloria.

When Gloria joined the congregation for worship one Sunday, the pastor was in the middle of the message when Gloria called out and needed support. The congregation gasped and recoiled, and no one knew how to intervene. The pastor called an audible and patched the situation from the pulpit with a quick conversation, but it was clear to everyone that they needed a plan. An individual was quickly appointed to fill the role of team coordinator and tasked with putting together a plan. She got to know Gloria and her parents. The next Sunday, the pastor let the congregation know that everyone could access written materials helpful for gaining knowledge and that the church would be hosting a speaker on the topic of mental health challenges within the next month at an adult education class.

Gloria came to the worship center with her parents and the coordinator on a Saturday to learn about some of the ins and outs of attending church, and the coordinator invited Gloria to sit with her and her family on Sunday. A team of four other people were introduced to Gloria and her parents, welcoming Gloria to sit with one of them each week.

While there are still good days and bad days, Gloria and her parents know they have a community that understands their situation and is eager to embrace all three of them. The congregation no longer recoils on days Gloria calls out during worship, and the pastor enjoys the taking walking coffee breaks in the parking lot during the week. When Gloria does not show up on a Sunday, people miss her. It's clear that Gloria belongs.

15

Practical Tools for Your Congregation:

Useful for equipping your congregation in Responsive Design.

Program Intake Form

We suggest you gather basic contact information (name, birthdate, address, phone number, email), and the answers to these three questions:

1. Which programs, services, or opportunities do you wish to participate in (Sunday worship, midweek youth group, Bible study, etc.)?
2. What are some areas of strength of gifting you can share with us (drawing, writing, encouraging, reading, singing, attitude, social relationships, following rules, paying attention, technology, athletics, etc.)?
3. What are some areas of struggles and challenge within this environment that you can share with us (drawing, writing, encouraging, reading, attitude, paying attention, social relationships, following rules, technology, athletics—as well as allergies, medical needs, etc.)?

We have created a template for this intake form[36]. We include the photo release we use to gain permission to use photos and videos of participants within the form. Having photos and videos of people with

---

[36] See links at https://allbelong.org/worship-as-one.

varied abilities in all media is part of a great universal design plan (and fewer forms to fill out is always nice)!

"I Notice" Conversation Examples

1. Conversation between parent and Sunday school teacher:

I've been looking forward to talking with you. How I love having Micah in my class. She is amazing! She is so drawn to the Lego area each week. I have never seen a four-year-old build such elaborate and creative structures! The kids were gathered around her today just watching her build. She brightens our room with that amazing smile of hers! She also really enjoys goldfish. She's a great eater, and she always knows what to do with that cup and napkin when finished. I can see you really value great manners at home. I also noticed that when I ask her a question, I cannot understand many of her words. Have you noticed that?

Did you notice how many "green" areas the volunteer talked about? This teacher wanted the parents to know all the many special qualities in Micah. Did you notice how many "pink" areas the volunteer talked about? One. Just One. And it was noted as an observed behavior, not presumed to have a label. Notice the teacher did *not* say, "I noticed your child has a speech deficit." The teacher just described what was observed and followed it up by passing it back to the parent.

The parent then has two responses. One is to say, "Yes, I have noticed that" and then the teacher can talk about what kind of approach they are trying or ask if they have anyone who is spending some time supporting Micah. The conversation may lead to ideas to try at church.

The second would be to say, "No, I have not noticed that," and then it may be important to realize it truly may be the setting. Micah may be speaking just fine at home, but social pressure may be an issue.

There are so many possibilities. If this is the answer you receive, it's still good to come up with strategies. The teacher may want to say, "I wonder if I could learn from you as the parent. Could we talk about ways I could do more of what you do at home so Micah can be comfortable speaking here at church?"

With either response, you can have further conversations with the parent.

2. Conversation with an adult and the adult small group leader

Again, this conversation is based on the idea that you as the leader have noticed several of the "green" areas of strength and can talk to the adult about this. Then you bring up that one "pink" area.

I am so thankful to be part of a small group with you. Your insights about the book of John totally changed my prayer life last week. I noticed you articulate yourself so well and are thoughtful of our group by bringing in amazing home-baked goodies. Thank you. I also noticed you invite everyone out for lunch, even if it's your first time meeting that person. But that does make me concerned about your safety. Does that make sense to you?

That individual may say yes, which may give you opportunity to talk about or write a list of safe ways to connect with people in the group. That person may also say no, and at that point, it will be helpful to seek a better understanding of that person's perspective by asking more questions or pointing out that we see things differently. Perhaps there might be a time when you would ask another person to join the conversation and get their opinion.

Again, this type of conversation begins in a way surrounded by the beauty of that person's puzzle piece while still addressing some of the areas of concern.

Learning from the Family or Individual

We created a template for gathering critical information that has helped many congregations[37] but these questions can get you started.

- Where do you desire to engage in the life of the church right now? (Adult Bible study, Sunday School, Youth Group, Worship, missions' trip, etc.)
- Please list some strengths, hobbies, gifts and/or interests – What do you enjoy doing?
- Each person is a combination of areas of strength and of challenge. What is challenging for you?
- We would like to know more about your skills and abilities. Please share what you are comfortable with about the following areas:
    - Language (speaking, understanding, reading, writing)
    - Gross motor skills (such as walking, crawling, sitting, moving, etc.)
    - Self-care & social skills
    - Paying attention
    - Spiritual understanding and awareness
    - Emotional regulation (frustration level, sensitivity, etc.)
    - Sensation (sight, smell, sound, taste, touch, balance, body awareness

Do we have your permission to share this information with leaders of those ministries in order to support your involvement? (If necessary, a specific list of names can be given for who will receive this information, and/or with whom we can discuss what is shared.)

---

[37] Ibid.

Samples: Get to Know Me Document & Personalized Responsive Design Plan

On the following pages you will find samples of a "Get to Know Me" document, and a filled out Personalized Responsive Design Plan form. Templates are available[38] to download and edit. These are the documents you will be able to create with the information you gather from the individual and/or family.

The "Get to Know Me" document provides leaders, peers, and others quick and easy access to information about a person who they will be teaching, assisting, visiting, or otherwise interacting with. You may want everyone in a small group or class to have one! Always ensure the individual and/or family fill out the permission section, because you always need permission to share this information!

A Responsive Design Plan form is where you bring together information and ideas. The form has quadrants for sorting out how this individual will participate in worship, fellowship, education, and service. Notice that there is space for two sides of the plan: one for the individual and one for the congregation, in each of the four quadrants.

---

[38] Ibid.

GET TO KNOW ME DOCUMENT

Modify this to be true to the individual and family in your community.

GET TO KNOW: Maria

This document is considered confidential and is passed out to ___Maria___'s friends and group leaders with ___Maria___'s permission to help create a place of belonging for ___Maria___ and his/her friends to grow in Christ. The church asked the accessibility committee members to visit with ___Maria___ and family/caregiver(s). This is a summary based on that interaction.

___Maria___ participates in the life of ___Church___ through:
name of church/organization

Sunday morning services, Women's Bible Study, Wednesday night potluck

list events, programs, etc.

___Maria___'s story:

Maria is an adult woman who has spent most of the last twenty years in an adult foster care home next door to our church. When Maria was a child, her family took her to church with them, but when she moved to her home next to church, she did not have a way to attend a church. Maria made her wishes to attend church known to the staff members at her home, and they started to ask us questions about her attendance. Our church put together a team of four people (Megan, Drew, Carina, and Delaney) who learned more about how Maria communicates and how to safely offer her elements of the Lord's Supper and how to share a meal together at our potluck night. They also know more details about her wheelchair and how to best make sure she is heard when she expresses discomfort. We are delighted that Maria has chosen our congregation and look forward to seeing her group of four friends grow into a much larger set of people who can learn from Maria and support her as needed. Maria asks that we tell you she is willing to pray for you as needed, so feel free to mention your prayer requests to her at any point in time.

GET TO KNOW ME DOCUMENT

___Maria___'s interests and joys:

Being with people. She has been a music lover for many years and also takes seriously God's call on her life to pray for those in her community. Her smile brightens a room, and she really enjoys being with children.

list the "greens"

___Maria___'s areas of challenge:

Maria has voluntary control of her eyes only. She can answer yes or no questions by looking at you if the answer is yes and looking away from you if the answer is no. She is a wheelchair user who requires support with all aspects of daily life, such as eating, drinking, and using the bathroom. Maria's diagnosis: Cerebral Palsy.

list the "pinks" and if applicable, diagnosis

Want more information or to join ___Maria___'s community team? ___Maria___ is comfortable having you contact ___Megan, Drew, Carina, or Delaney___

contact person

to set up a time of introduction or to answer your questions and provide you with more information.

PERSONALIZED RESPONSIVE DESIGN PLAN

DATE: September 19, 2022

This plan is good for ___3___ weeks/(months) and will be re-viewed/updated on December 2022

Plan for Jay W. (name) **and** Northwood Church (name of church/ministry/organization)

SETTING	PLAN FOR INDIVIDUAL	PLAN FOR CONGREGATION
IN WORSHIP	Jay can use sound blockers during singing, and also take breaks by enjoying worship in the quiet room off the main hallway where he can control the sound level piped in from the worship center. Jay has a job to do during greeting time in the service. Jay has access to fidgets and wiggle seats in the worship center during the message and is encouraged to draw in his sketchbook as well.	Announcements about the availability of sound blockers and earplugs raise awareness that they may be needed by some individuals. There are multiple sets for anyone to use, and one is always available for Jay. The preacher/presenter can ask Jay to come prepare for the message when releasing others to greet one another. (see service plan) If the preacher/presenter will be including music, video, or something loud, it is helpful to give Jay a warning that it is coming (which can be done when planning the visuals/props).
IN EDUCATION	Jay will participate in the Sunday school hour, taking his sketchbook along. He may sit with the group or at a table to the side of the group if he chooses. He may take advantage of up to four break tickets during the hour—to take breaks as needed. Jay will know that each break lasts two minutes, as designated on the Time Timer, and can include getting a drink, walking the halls, or reading the poster on the bulletin board without going into other rooms.	A general understanding of the variety of sensory differences in people and about ASD needs to be shared regularly with Sunday school leaders. Jay's classmates need to know the break ticket plan, and the head of Sunday school can ensure that Jay is following the plan when taking breaks.
IN FELLOWSHIP	During the fellowship time between the Sunday school hour and the worship service. Refreshments served must include a gluten-free option for Jay.	One of the tables in the fellowship hallway used during the fellowship time will be saved for Jay and two of his classmates from Sunday school. These peers will learn about Jay's gifts and needs and take turns enjoying this time with him.
IN SERVICE	Jay is a part of the worship team in a unique way. During greeting time, Jay has a job to do (which helps him avoid greetings). He gathers the items, images, and so forth that the preacher/presenter for that day will be using and gets them on the stage, checking in with the sound booth to ensure that props and visuals are all in place for the message.	Sound booth, worship band members and preacher/presenter need to know Jay's role and method of communicating—mostly thumbs-up/down or jumps signifying happy/yes, head shaking signifying no, and rocking motion signifying he is getting upset.

Community Team Questionnaires

If you know or suspect you will be forming a team around the individual or family you are gathering information from, you will want to add information and questions particular to creating the team[39]. This team may be part of the Responsive Design Plan. Team members will greatly appreciate a « Get to Know Me » page on the individual or family. You will need to ask potential team members some questions as well. The type of team and who is on it may depend on the situation, and some or all of these questions can be used to put together a team.

For the individual or family who will be the Heart of the Team:

We want to wrap around you/your family as the Body of Christ, in order to support you right now. The information you provide here will be used to build a team of people who will support you in the ways you indicate are most needed, who will pray for you and come alongside you through this time. Once a team is set up, we will have a gathering where you can share your story if you wish, your greatest needs and your hopes and fears. The team may change over time, and your needs may change, and this document may no longer be the best place to have the information but serves as a starting place to form a plan. The Team Leader(s) will connect with you about what is shared here and together you can agree upon a plan.

- What do you look forward to most about having a Community Team?
- What concerns you about having a Community Team?
- What do you see as the aim or goal of this team?
- What is the best way to communicate your needs on a regular basis (Email, phone, text, etc.)?

---

[39] Ibid.

- How long do you think this Community Team should be in place? (It's ok to not know right now!)
- Who might we ask to be a part of your team? (Prospective team members may come from within the church, in the family, or other connections. They may not all necessarily have to be local.)
- Are there names of people we should be aware of that you would prefer are NOT added to the team or its communication?
- Would you like support with …?
    - ☐ Transportation
    - ☐ Participating in church activities (please give specifics)
    - ☐ Social opportunities
    - ☐ Meals at home
    - ☐ Household care (laundry, housekeeping, etc.)
    - ☐ Yardwork/upkeep
    - ☐ Paperwork (filling out, filing, submitting, understanding, etc.)
    - ☐ Medical and other appointments (taking notes, understanding instructions, handling paperwork, etc.)
    - ☐ Other: _____
- Is there equipment the support team could or should use to help you in the above listed ways, if they learned how to? How might they learn to use it?

For Prospective Team Members:

- What brings you to this Team?
- Do you live nearby?
- What skills and gifts are you willing to bring to the Team to support this individual/family? *(sewing, cleaning, socializing, patient listening, baking, driving, taking notes, finances, coordinating with team members, e.g.)*
- What tasks will you NOT do? *(change diapers, mow the lawn, e.g.)*
- Are there tasks that would be difficult for you? *(Such as lifting things heavier than 30 pounds)*
- If those difficult tasks are things you would like to do, how can the Team help you participate in that way? *(For example, you want to make meals, but don't drive and ask that someone else help you bring the meals)*
- What else should the Team Leader (the "Central Nervous System") know? *(Such as, you have young children and therefore plans can change quickly, or your job can cause you to travel and may interrupt communication or participation for periods of time)*
- What's the best way to reach you if something is urgent?

You'll also want to have their name, relationship to "the heart", contact information and availability.

Part 4: The 3-Part Plan in Action

This section is intended to give you a very practical application for this 3-part plan: perspective (puzzle pieces), participation (universal design), and personalization (responsive design). While we could look at this 3-part plan in the context of every possible ministry of the church, I will only highlight what this planning process might look like as sprinkled (just like the "shredded cheese" model) into the infant and toddler ministry, children and youth ministry, and worship ministry. The information is not intended to be exhaustive, but my hope is that you will read through several ideas to get your own creative juices flowing.

16

The 3-Part Plan in Infant & Toddler Ministry

Puzzle Piece Perspective

Perspective through diagnosis

One of the first times parents and a congregation encounter the opportunity to have a puzzle piece perspective is when they discover their child may have some type of disability or difference. This can happen at three distinct times, and the response of the parents and the church can be different during each one of those times. In each situation, both the parents and the congregation may need to be enfolded into the beauty of the puzzle piece perspective. In keeping with what the Rev. Dr. LaTonya Penny says about radical hospitality, the church must be ready to fight cultural and historical attitudes that would deny this child participation in the life of the community.[40]

First, a parent may find out *before a child is born* **that their child has some type of difference or disability.** Various screens and tests that are part of prenatal care can highlight the possibility of a different area of development. Parents, for example, may know that their child will be born with Down syndrome or spina bifida. In fact, some children have procedures done prior to birth, given the information the medical team has gained. In some cases, parents have been given a strong suggestion to terminate the pregnancy.

---

[40] See Rev. Dr. LaTonya Penny, "Universal Design for Worship: Introductory Reflections," Durham, NC, August 4, 2018.

It's difficult to go against a trusted doctor or medical professional, so how can the church weigh in with a different perspective and support a parent who has to make this decision? How can the knitting process the psalmist writes about in Psalm 139 be an important factor in making this choice? A congregation that is going to be pro-life at this point in the journey also needs to be ready to be pro-life as the child is welcomed, enfolded, and grows. As parents are enfolded into a congregation that sees the gifts of each person, is ready to support the areas of challenge, and knows the valuable contribution this child will make to the community, the boldness to say yes to a full-term pregnancy becomes even a greater possibility. While I am fully aware that areas of need and challenge for some children will require the support of the congregational village to live and thrive, what a gift a community offers when there is overwhelming confidence that this child will be used by God and blessed by God!

If a parent and congregation know that a child will have some type of disability before birth, they have an opportunity to get ready. Learn along with the parents about that area of disability. Think about and study together the puzzle piece perspective. Learn from other families who already have a child with this type of difference. If parents are okay with letting the congregation know in advance, stock some books in your library for congregation members to check out. Organize an adult education session on the topic. Equip your community to receive this little one with information as well as the open arms a puzzle piece perspective requires.

It may also be wise to arrange to have a response team ready once when the birth takes place. Will the parents need help and support for other children in their home? Can a meal plan be set up? Parents will be busy once the child is born and having layers of support set up will speak volumes about the church's commitment. Make sure to include a way to introduce this new congregational puzzle piece to your community.

It's important to mention that parents will very likely need time to work through the reality of this difference in their new family member. The diagnosis wasn't what they were expecting, and this new reality requires listening ears around them that can hear the grief and pain of altered expectations and, as Jolene Philo puts it, a different dream for their child.[41] Adopting a puzzle piece perspective does not minimize the process important to these parents—and for all of us—in a life-changing event. Yet the joy and peace that come from knowing their child will be embraced by those who are able to see the treasure and gift of this little one is a way to foster encouragement and promote healing.

Second, a parent may find out *at birth* that a child has some type of difference or disability. A birth trauma may have caused something like a stroke in the infant during birth or the child was without oxygen and now is known to have cerebral palsy. It's also possible that pregnancy tests did not pick up this area of difference. In any event, the parents and congregation enter into this news as a sudden surprise. There is not time before the child's arrival to prepare for the unique needs that often accompany such a diagnosis. They were not expecting a member of the Down syndrome society to show up at the hospital. The parents were not imagining having to leave their child in an intensive care unit. The congregation was not expecting this news.

In this case, parents have expressed the need to adjust, but not within the context of sympathy. Sending a quick text or email is often preferred. Telling a parent that you will be bringing a meal over on Thursday as opposed to saying "Let me know if I can do anything" is often much appreciated. Having the congregation offer support and a glimpse of the puzzle piece perspective in texts, emails, and limited

---

[41] Jolene Philo, *A Different Dream for My Child: Meditations for Parents of Critically or Chronically Ill Children* (Grand Rapids: Discovery House, 2009).

visits will be a terrific way to walk with this family. Find ways to get information about the area of disability, but trade this off quickly for a chance to get to know the child. Remember, this is not Cerebral Palsy Nate. This is Nate, with eyes like his mom's eyes, who is nursing well or poorly, who was stoic through twenty-eight hours of labor, who will be used by God to grow the community, who also happens to have cerebral palsy. It's important to have a liaison between the church and the parents and it's usually best if this person is already in relationship with the family. While this may change over time to the inclusion coordinator, begin with a person they know and trust as you build the bridge to walking with the child, the family, and with your community in placing this newborn puzzle piece into the congregational jigsaw frame.

Third, a parent may find out *after birth* that a child has some type of difference or disability. This discovery could take place a couple months after birth when the child's muscles aren't working on the same timeline as other two-month-olds. It may be when the child is in day care and isn't using words at the age of three. It may be many years later when a school suggests an evaluation because of learning or social skill issues. It may be as an adult when they are diagnosed with depression or have had an injury or accident that caused a physical difference.

While many scenarios are possible, the impact for churches seems generally similar. The individual is probably a child or adult who is already part of your programs. You may or may not have noticed some of these challenges. Whatever the case, you have the distinct opportunity to walk beside the parents and the individual as they go through this time of discovery or evaluation.

It can be a scary time for some. For others, it may be a relief to finally get a "name" for some of the differences they have noticed. Whatever the reaction, it calls on the beauty of the puzzle piece perspective in powerful ways. I often say to parents as they enter a season of testing and evaluation, "Remember, the child you put to bed on Tuesday—the one you know and love—is the very same child you will put to bed on Wednesday—the one you now have some more information about due to the results of an evaluation. You are still that child's expert. That child is still an amazing and dearly loved child of God, and now you may have some additional direction on how best to parent and raise your child. This process may lead you to strategies to try." It's important for parents and individuals to have people who can walk with them and remind them of who that child is! Find ways to share the journey.

Another important reminder is that many children who are diagnosed after birth fall into the category called "hidden disabilities." When a child uses a wheelchair or sports the facial characteristics of a child with Down syndrome, people see the disability immediately. For many individuals, however, that area of difference is not readily seen by others. I've often heard parents say, "I wish my child had some sort of sign that says, 'I have a disability,' so that people could better interpret what they see." In fact, some parents and children experience great judgment as "you're a bad parent" or "this child is just being naughty."

While you may not take extraordinary joy in telling everyone that your child has a significant lack of the neurotransmitter dopamine and therefore finds sitting still for any length of time biologically impossible, it beats the alternative of being labeled "naughty," "out of control," "just like his uncle," or "the result of bad parents."

Regardless of when parents find out about their child having some sort of difference or disability, the question for us as Christ's body is this: How can we embrace *each individual* as a valuable part of our congregational puzzle with gifts to share and challenges we can support?

Puzzle Piece Perspective through announcements, visits, and cards.

While parents will need time to adjust to their new reality, the congregation and parents can benefit from information supplied through a puzzle piece perspective. When making the birth announcement, make sure you let people know that the parents gave birth to a *baby* and not a disability! Remember who that baby is— God's child handknit by God in God's image—as you make the announcement. This is not a death announcement; it's a *birth* announcement.

When you visit the family, remember that you're encouraging parents who had a *baby*, not a disability. There is so much more to talk about than the challenges facing the baby. We can talk about the color of the baby's eyes, the length of labor and delivery, the colors of the nursery, the way the child's nose resembles another family member. While the conversation will undoubtedly include the reality of the disability, we must be aware that the whole picture is something much, much larger.

When you send a card, text, or email, consider the experience that Adam's mom and dad had with their neighbor Don when they came home from the hospital with Adam as a newborn. Don seemed to understand puzzle pieces. Please know that this conversation happened after a doctor had referred to Adam as "it" and suggested the parents forget the birth ever happened and leave without "it," after the nurses had taken their name off the new parents dinner list because they assumed they wouldn't want to be with the "happy" parents, and after several people had mailed them sympathy cards. Imagine, then, the puzzle piece joy in this conversation:

Then, without sympathy or pity, Don said, 'My wife and I have read what we could find on Down syndrome to be better able to welcome Adam into the neighborhood. Is there anything we should read or do to support you and Jetta?" "I wish people would just treat us all like normal, new parents and treat our son, Adam, whom we loved and wanted, like the one-week-old baby he is." . . . I later learned that after our visit with Don, he and Val talked to everyone in the neighborhood explaining our desire to continue just being ourselves and our desire to remove the word special from describing our son. They restated the greeting to: "Please welcome Jetta and David's son Adam whom they are celebrating!"[42]

Participation: Universal Design

Here are some important tools to think through as you prepare your welcome for the infants and toddlers. Please note you should have already addressed safety features for both equipment and volunteers. The importance of areas such as cleanliness and volunteer screening should be in place in all congregations.

- Consider meeting with each new set of parents to establish a relationship, offer support, and begin to have discussions about what they have already noticed about their child's greens and pinks. Use the questions and forms from chapter 15.
- Line up a volunteer whose role is to observe in the infant and toddler areas. The early childhood volunteers in a church are often the ones who will notice some differences in a child. Having someone you can call on who has experienced eyes trained in this area can be a huge support to the staff and parents. This person may be able to answer the question, "Is this difference within a typical range for a child this age?" This person may be able to give ideas for supporting this child or even suggest the formation of a responsive design plan.

---

[42] David Winstrom, *I Choose Adam: Nothing Special Please* (Denver, CO: Lightning Tree Creative Media, 2017), 68.

- Provide a list to all volunteers in your 0-3-year-old areas that gives typical levels of development for children this age. While it isn't the church's job to diagnose a child (we must be very careful to not do this), it is helpful to share information about what is typical and what is not in terms of development. This basic knowledge can provide clues for knowing when it may be wise to speak with a parent.
- Develop a list of trusted local resources parents can use for evaluation purposes. Speak to congregation members who may know medical doctors, psychologists, therapists, and specialty centers in the area they would trust to come alongside parents and support them with a puzzle piece perspective. While you may use this list as part of a responsive design plan, compiling it and having it ready to go is a great universal design feature.
- Plan for different preferences. When you are stocking supplies and setting up areas, consider the differences children may have. Some will thrive in the middle of an active group. Others will want access to a quiet area with fewer noises and interruptions. Provide a variety of ways and places that children can sit that are appropriate to age levels. Having small, stable chairs with arms, as well as beanbags and carpet squares, may be a great start. Adding adult- and child-sized rocking chairs can also be helpful. Open areas and protected spots, places with a large number of toys and places that feature a limited number of toys, staffing where one adult can supervise several children and a place where one adult can safely spend time with one or two children, brighter areas and calming, dimly lighted areas—all of these can be among the options for the youngest ones. Children already come wired with many differences, even at these early ages. Giving options within your space can be helpful.
- Stock up on resource books and trainings. Make sure you, your volunteers, and your parents have access to resources about those areas of disability that impact children at these age levels. The

resources shared at the back of this book can give you a place to begin.

Personalization: Responsive Design

It's important that the process for a personalized responsive design plan be in motion and ready to implement in the infant and toddler area of your congregation.

Parents of young children may have no idea that developmental differences exist. This may be their first child. A trusted person may have downplayed some of the differences, so parents have dismissed them as unimportant. In many cases, the people who staff your 0-3-year-old areas may be the first to notice a difference. Get ready to use your pair of eyes and resource charts to decide if it's time to have a conversation with a parent.

Remember that it's not the job of the church to *diagnose* a child. There are times, however, when noticing an area of challenge will allow a child to get support in the crucial years of brain development. For example, if you suspect a hearing loss, that loss may be easily corrected but can also cause significant issues for speech and language development. In addition, a child who shows early signs of autism spectrum disorder can gain access to powerful early childhood supports totally covered by insurance. Early intervention is extremely important for many, so be discerning about when it may be time to talk to a parent.

Early childhood intervention is important, but it's also valuable to remember that this is a journey for parents who may not have known before or at birth that there was an area of disability. I often suggest to people who surround the parents that they consider this journey a bit like a book. Some have information that has allowed them to know several of the chapters in this child's diagnostic book. The parents, however, may not have even had the chance to pick up the book up or know there is one. Make sure you journey together with parents as you travel through the book. Hand it to them gently, covering it in prayer and asking for the Holy Spirit's leading.

Children change quickly. A child may need a plan for a year and then be developmentally back on track. They may mature. They may receive therapy that levels out challenging behavior. You may need to reassure parents that a personalized plan is about giving supports so their child can be successful. It may be needed for a brief time or for a long time, and their child's presence in the community is totally worth the effort!

Learning From Congregations:

- Once you know that a child will benefit from a responsive design plan, get ready to be creative. Use your resources to follow the process described in part 3. Here are some creative ways congregations have responded to the gifts and challenges of infants and toddlers:
- One community knew that the child would be at risk physically if placed in a church nursery, so they set up an around-church community team. They trained 4 people within the church to rotate going to that child's home during worship each week, so parents and other family members could attend the gathering.
- Another community had the space to have a nurse who staffed a small nursery for those little ones whose health conditions made them vulnerable to many things. They had two children who needed medical supervision and so they responded by creating that option for these two children.
- One child had been having seizures. Parents worked with the inclusion coordinator to come up with an emergency plan, which was then communicated to all workers and placed on the wall. As part of the plan, parents were given a walkie-talkie that allowed them to be reached quickly if necessary.

- One child didn't yet have a diagnosis, but he was biting other children in the two-year-old setting. Remember, your community *will* include children who will get a diagnosis much later in life. Also, there may be some children who just need extra support at this age. You can use your responsive design ideas for any child who needs something personalized in place to be successful. A child may be biting for just a season, or they may enter an evaluation phase and discover it's part of a set of behaviors that make up a diagnosis. For now, this child needs support. This church recruited an extra set of volunteers who were to serve as a shield to the other children should he choose to bite. These volunteers functioned as a community team, though they chose to operate two-weeks-on, two-weeks-off, with two volunteers who got to know this child well. A calming area was set up for those days when parents or the volunteers suspected things could be a little rough. The calming area was stocked with items the volunteers could use with him, which often helped him become less frustrated so he could return to the group.

17

The 3-Part Plan in Children & Youth Ministry

Puzzle Piece Perspective

Interacting with parents is an excellent time to communicate the puzzle piece perspective. What questions you ask first often tell a lot about your perspective. From the minute I meet a parent who has a child with a disability, I want that parent to know I see a child first. Consider the green and pink puzzle pieces as you read through two options in a discussion with parents.

Option 1: "Hi. I'm going to be Yolanda's Sunday school teacher. What's wrong with her anyway?"

Option 2: "Hi. I'm going to be Yolanda's Sunday school teacher. Can you tell me some of the things she loves to do?"

As you can tell, option 1 starts with the pink areas, while option 2 starts with the green areas. Can you feel the difference? Parents of children with disabilities are almost always surrounded by pink conversations. They are told how many degrees below zero, how atypical, how dysfunctional, how many percentage points below . . . We, however, don't need to share that perspective! God has given us a puzzle piece perspective through which to view that child. I want parents to know from the first time I meet them that I see Yolanda, hand-knit by God in His image with gifts to share and areas of challenge to support, just like every other child in our children's ministry. I want them to know that Yolanda's puzzle piece fits well within the heart of our community. She belongs.

The puzzle piece perspective may help you set up opportunities within children's and youth ministry. I am aware that many communities set up a separate option for children and youth with disabilities, but I ask you to please consider some important parts of the puzzle piece picture as you evaluate your supports. Consider especially that puzzle pieces join together to influence all the other pieces. We fit together like a puzzle in the body of Christ.

The presence of a child with a disability is a puzzle piece that will touch those gathered around them. Many children attend schools where they have classmates with disabilities who are part of the activities and friendships. Community sports teams, library gatherings, and park offerings typically welcome children and youth of all abilities. If, however, a child comes to church and the response is to routinely separate out each peer with some kind of disability and send that person to "Room 7" or "Special Treasures" or some other segregated area, the peers will learn quickly that not every piece of the puzzle fits within their group. But if your first choice is to have that child or youth be part of the community that has a personalized plan to support that person, the children will grow up understanding that church is also a place where we fit together as puzzle pieces. They will learn how to include their friend in a Bible study and how to respond when that friend has a good day or when they have a rough day.

Remember, you are raising future leaders of the church who will be small group leaders and pastors and Sunday school teachers and litany writers for the Easter service. How difficult will it be for a set of peers to make sure Rachel has a part in the litany because that is what they have practiced since childhood? How easy will it be to invite her to an adult small group and employ her gifts in God's service and learn from her? They have been doing that since they were children. Remember, a segregated area is teaching not only the individuals in that space but also the peers who watch people be ushered into that space.

I want to make it clear that it's still important to make individual decisions. My advice to congregations is always to "preserve the body" as much as possible. Keep people in the same space and actively growing in their faith together. Look for materials and curriculums that are put together with features of the universal design vision. The options are built in. If not, add those into your curriculums. There are situations, however, where being together with peers of all abilities may not be possible for an entire session or year. More important than shoving people into *programs*, it's important to get to know the individual, with the help of a responsive design plan, and make decisions about how they can best worship, learn more about Jesus, interact with others, and use their gifts in God's service. Build around individuals, and you will be delighted how the community can form within natural age groups. Consider "Room 7" as one option for part of the time *only* after exhausting other options. Be creative in keeping the community together.

Learning From Congregations

Consider some examples from congregations as they put together options in children and youth ministry.

1. Wheaton, Illinois

A church in Wheaton, Illinois, had two small spaces designated for children with varied abilities. The inclusion coordinator spent her week producing adapted materials in bins that buddies could take to the children's rooms and use to help the child interact with the lesson of the day. One of the smaller spaces was set up as a vibrantly decorated space filled with a sand table, mini trampoline, rocking chair, art area, and a few other key items to allow buddies to use that area when a child needed a "reset" time and a "break" from the main area. The other space was dimly lit and quiet, with only a few chairs for sitting and a few bins available to pull out as needed.

Justin spent the entire time in that space because of stimulation challenges. The coordinator had tried other options, but Justin communicated clearly through his screams that those weren't working for him. The quiet area allowed him to be present at church, and his parents to participate in worship. Even in the reality of Justin's situation, it's important to note that the other children knew him well. They had a prayer area with his picture in it. The leader of that fourth-grade group would text his mom for prayer requests, and then as a group they would text prayer requests back to his mom for prayer at home during the week. Sometimes Justin and his church buddy would make baggies of treats to pass out in the other room, and kids would make cards and special items for Justin. Though they weren't able to be in the same physical space yet, they knew each other well, and they gave and received to each other in a variety of ways. When Justin arrived at church, several kids greeted him by name. He could receive their welcome and return it in a way unique to him. His peers were unafraid of his responses, and he was part of the community, despite the physical distance. This church "preserved the body" in a unique way.

2. Holland, Michigan

A church in Holland, Michigan, noticed that one individual in their youth group was being left out. She had some differently wired social skills and behaviors that were distancing her from her peers. The youth group leaders knew that everyone would grow if they better equipped them with information to help them understand God's unique wiring in each group member. Using the puzzle piece lesson plan (see chapter 6), they set up a time for each person to learn about their wiring and then made a wall display showing how they fit together like a puzzle in the body of Christ.

The leader highlighted many individuals, but especially made note of Ashley's puzzle piece. Group members were encouraged to adopt as a goal to make sure that the wall display of interconnected puzzle pieces did not have any dangling pieces. The group did well for a few weeks, and when the leaders noticed Ashley's piece dangling, the group brainstormed ideas and solutions. Every youth group member grew that year. This youth group highly prized their community puzzle picture and came up with specific ways to keep the community growing, learning, and serving one another.

The puzzle piece perspective allows you to look for the green stitching in each young person, which is an especially powerful thought as you put together opportunities for your groups. Most of us enjoy spending time interacting with our greens. In general, we tolerate or avoid the pink areas. Imagine, then, how difficult it can be in youth group if social skills are a pink area? Imagine if tolerating loud noises are a pink area? You would want to find greener pastures for that individual so church meetings and visits would be experienced as pleasant! For me, if the church program was made up of just ball games all the time where I was forced to play, it may take me two tries before I develop Sunday illnesses, excuses, and finally refusal. If, however, my delight in words, music, and word games are woven into and between the ball games, I would tolerate the sporting events to enjoy my green areas.

Apply that to someone you know who may be having a tough time tolerating a children's or youth program. Can you find out what is green for that person? Perhaps an individual would love to be there if he could bring a picture each week to feature in a frame on the wall. Displaying his artwork may bring him boundless joy and allow him to tolerate some of the other areas. Another person may enjoy having a five-minute conversation with a designated person each week about an episode of *Star Trek*. Imagine a person who is green in memory and is asked to memorize and then recite a passage of Scripture or other text for the group each week. What about a child who loves to give high fives? Could this person be a permanent greeter into the meeting area? Look for those green areas. Give opportunities for a person to enter that green time in each gathering. In many cases, I've watched people eventually look forward to even the pink areas of gatherings because the green brings joy and performs a valuable service to others in the group. While it's dangerous for this woman from Michigan to utter these words, I say, "Go Green!"

Participation Universal Design

Hang on, and don't get overwhelmed as you think about participation. Remember, this is a starting point for thinking about procedures and equipment to put in place as way to provide options. This is not just an isolated response to an individual with a disability; it's a way to honor all the children and youth in your community. These ideas are available and applicable to 100 percent of the community, even though the applications may be more heavily used by certain people in that community during certain seasons of time.

This section is divided into three parts: preparation work, meet and greet, and in-room supports and procedures. All Belong knows the value of having hands-on tools to help make this happen.

Universal Design and Preparation Work:

First, look around your community. Have there been ample opportunities to communicate the puzzle piece perspective to the community as a whole? Does your community support and understand the importance of creating spaces for persons of all abilities? Has your pastor put this vision in front of the congregation? One reason this is important: it's your volunteer pool. Our children and youth programs rely on volunteers. If leadership has cast the vision to the group, the options will make a lot more sense to your volunteers. Also, children and youth should be ready to receive the gifts that each person brings. Are they equipped to know the wide variety in God's knitting patterns? Has this vision been specifically taught to them? If not, read the supports for the puzzle piece chapter and see if some of those insights can be implemented as soon as possible.

Offer ways for children and youth to "visit" the programs ahead of time. Many of us look for information before we visit a hotel or other location. We look online, hoping there is a picture or video tour that will tell us more about what food is served, whether there is a pool, what reviews people have given the hotel, if there is an extra cost for parking or internet, and what the room layout is. Think about the information you are looking for and see if there is a way to communicate it on your church website or in a printed booklet prior to the beginning of the church year. I call this a church welcome story. Let parents and children explore the offerings together, just like they would visit other sites on the internet together. Let them see the faces of the people they will meet, introduce them to the format of the time together, show some of the past pictures of youth group events or children's ministry gatherings. Again, online is great, but printed booklets can be helpful as well.

Another wonderful option is to offer pre-visits for the children and youth. Ask leaders to staff their areas and invite parents and children to come for a visit so they can explore the area, meet the people, and even take some photos of kids and leaders together to practice learning names and the environment before you begin. An open house is a terrific way to allow people to explore the space with the leaders, without adding the social pressure of peers and expectations.

Offer training to your leaders. Are your volunteers expecting to be with children of all abilities? Have you spent any time giving them information geared to helping them understand some of the children who may be part of their groups, and are you giving them tools for supporting the children?

Develop registration forms that reflect the puzzle piece design. Consider adapting or using the intake form (see chapter 15) to help you collect information on each child or youth who is part of your program. Doing so will signal parents that each child in your community has areas of gifts and challenges and that all are welcome.

Be ready and embed a process so that you have a personalized responsive design plan in place. While the actual responsive design section comes next and the planning is part of that portion, a good universal design feature is that you have the process in place. When it's needed, you know who is in charge. When you review your registration forms and notice a family that warrants a phone call, you know who will make that call.

Universal Design and Meet and Greet Time

While some parents have accessible parking placards, others find that parking at church can be a big challenge. Their child may struggle to cross the parking lot safely or may find the entrance to your children or youth area loud and frightening. Think about the logistics of the entry to your children and youth area. It may be possible to designate "access parking—by invitation only" to some spots close to the door where children or youth may enter. You can assign these special parking passes to parents who may benefit from those close spots. Another option is to create a "sensory-friendly entrance" to your area. It may be a second option for an entrance, or entry through the main door may be managed with a lower noise level and with expectations that all will enter quietly and slowly.

If you have visitors, make sure they have an opportunity to give you the necessary information about their child in green and pink in a format similar to the registration form. Are you asking for this information in a way they will be comfortable sharing it, or are you asking verbally in front of many people or even in front of their children with listening ears? Think through the process you use and see if there should be changes or other options embedded. Remember that the parent's ability may also vary. You may encounter some who are unable to do the required reading and writing and would like an interview option. Remember, adults come with varied abilities as well.

Be ready with some people you can quickly call in as buddies. This may be the only position they fill in children or youth ministry. Some individuals may be comfortable coming alongside a child with unique wiring until you've worked through a responsive design plan. Think of asking people who may work in special education, serve as a therapist, or therapy assistant, or have experience as parents of children with disabilities. These individuals can be excellent choices for the "insta-buddy" position.

Universal Design and In-Room Supports and Procedures

In addition to a well-researched curriculum that provides embedded options for your children or youth setting, consider the following ideas:

1. Pictures

There are so many ways to use pictures. They can be turned into a visual schedule that will allow children to see the order of the day. They may also be paired with words for those who are readers. Remember, not every child does well with times written on a schedule. If you are even a minute behind the printed time, some children may struggle with the fact that you are not "on schedule." Remove the times and use a sequence of events.

Another way to use pictures is to give an option to children who would rather point to a picture for an answer than give it verbally. Consider ordering a second set of take-home pages or individual booklets and cutting up some pictures and illustrations. It will allow you to ask questions such as "Who is your favorite character in the story?" or "What is the best part of the story?" Pictures can allow you to make a prayer request, choose a song, or tell the group what you are thankful for. They can also be used in displays by lamination and attaching Velcro to the back of the picture.

2. Tools for Varied Sensory Systems

You will find a more detailed description of varied sensory systems in a few of the other books I have written (such as *Autism and Your Church* and *Accessible Gospel, Inclusive Worship*), but this quick description here emphasizes the need to prepare for children who demonstrate great variation in the way they process information through their senses. In fact, for some children, one of the most challenging times comes when their bodies are flooded with the hormones that are part of puberty, and they will show great variation in how they process this.

For the sake of a quick explanation, consider a ring tone on a phone. Some people may hear the ring tone but dismiss it without even thinking about it because it's not *their* ring tone. The noise is there, but the brain focuses on other things because what they're receiving is unimportant information. For another person, this ring tone is piercing or very loud. The person wants to cover their ears because it's painful. Another individual may be unable to register that tone. While their "hearing" is fine, it takes much larger doses of the noise to penetrate their brain. Three people and three different responses to the same noise. Who is correct? Since your own brain processes sensory input, *everyone* is correct. It's an individual thing that demonstrates variation.

Let's move the ring tone analogy into the places where children and youth gather in your setting for singing. I'm guessing some people join the worship and consider the sound level just fine. Everything falls in a "normal" range for that person. Another individual may head for the door with ears covered because the noise is way too loud and painful. Another person may move to the front and crave even more sound and volume. Again, who is right? Each one is correct, as each individual's brain is uniquely interpreting the sound.

The sensory system, however, is way more than sound. It can include sensations that help determine pain, temperature, balance, touch, taste, sight, and smell. Churches can be a minefield to children and youth who have sensitivities in one or more areas of the sensory system.

Before defeat settles into your own worldview, before you wonder how on earth you can possibly make everyone's sensory system happy, let me tell you that you can stock many items that will make a big difference for the children and youth in your setting:

- Sound blockers that children can borrow or use.
- Fidget pencils or "hand tools" that are part of each setting.
- Options for seating that provide movement, such as Hokki stools, wiggle cushions, beanbags, rocking chairs, or chairs with arms.
- "Break tickets"—a chance to grab a ticket and leave without having to verbally request to leave that setting. The break area, established in advance, can allow the child's sensory system to be reset.
- Lap buddies that are weighted, which small children can hold during circle time (a great source is large stuffed animals from which the stuffing has been pulled out and replaced with rice or plastic pellets).
- Items you discover that are helpful to an individual child and provided by a parent. These may include items a child can chew or hold.

In general, a person with a sensory difference will often self-medicate. Watch what they are doing and then provide an alternative that is okay with you. For example, if the child is rubbing their hands all over friends or leaders, you may want to give that child a fidget to hold. If a youth member is constantly on the move during times when others are quiet and seated, you may want to give them a large exercise ball or a Hokki stool to sit on. If a child is chewing on his clothing and making holes, consider giving them a coffee stirrer to chew or a commercially made item such as chewelry. The child's actions will tell you what they are craving or avoiding, and there are many ways to supply an alternative that works well within your setting.

In general, please consider that many children will struggle with worship bands and music projected at high volume. It is an act of kindness to find out what safe decibel levels are and commit to keeping your worship time within these levels.

3. Fine Motor Tools

If you use writing, cutting, coloring, or drawing as part of your activities, consider stocking a variety of tools. One size does not fit all these days, and children will choose what makes sense for them. You will want to have pencil grips, varied sizes of pencils and scissors, crayons that are both large and small, and tools that offer options to those who may prefer them. Again, you are not assigning one pencil to one person, but having them available allows a child to choose what works best. Since you want to encourage variation, consider asking parents or children what they use in school settings and stock those things. If you have older children, fidget pencils will be a great option. Again, consult All Belong's "best practices in a bag" for fidgets for attention, as well as an introduction to tools for supporting reading and writing.

4. Multisensory Options

If your curriculum already builds in multisensory options, you are all set. But great universal design uses a variety of ways to get information in and out. You may be telling a Bible story, but adding pictures adds another way for people to take in information. You may be giving a message to the youth but adding PowerPoint slides with visuals adds another way for people to take in the information. Adding an item for people to touch as you talk about that item as part of your verbal and visual message gives yet another point of access to the teaching of the day. In addition, if you allow people to respond to the message with a verbal discussion, that's one idea. If you add the option of making a poster or using pictures or objects to respond to the idea, you create another pathway for expression. If options aren't provided in your curriculum, add them to better embrace all people gathered.

In addition to those tools, consider checking out the following items:

- Time Timer—a great visual timer that allows people to watch the time disappear in a color format rather than a ticking format
- YouVersion—an excellent Bible app that quickly puts Scripture in front of you but also has a text-to-speech feature that is excellent; they also offer a version for children with interactive Bible stories
- Choice Works—a great app from beevisual.com for building individual or group schedules quickly and flexibly

Personalization: Responsive Design

It's important to have ready a responsive design plan to implement in the children and youth area of your congregation. There are factors and common issues unique to this age group. Just in case you skipped over it, it would be good to read the section on infant and toddler ministries, where you can find valuable information about how congregational involvement differs based on when a parent finds out a child has some sort of difference or disability. Children who are diagnosed with "hidden" disabilities will often go through that diagnosing process while they are already attending your programs. Parents may be asked to go through evaluations, and you may have the honor of walking with them through those uncertain and sometimes frightening times. I have covered much of that information in the previous section, so please make sure you are aware of those issues.

The issue of sensory processing differences can become more significant as bodies grow, change, and release hormones. Children who may have been comfortable in the children's area are now experiencing intense growth and change that may kick off differences in how medications are tolerated and light a fire under sensory differences that have been under control for several years. Some of the same tools that were helpful in younger years (noise blockers, fidgets, weighted backpacks, break areas, schedules, timers, and so forth) may be needed for a period of time again to help support the changes. An occupational therapist in your congregation or someone who works in a related field may have ideas that will be helpful to the youth, parents, and leaders during that time.

Leaders of evening events need to be aware of medications, especially the ones that treat the symptoms of attention deficit/hyperactivity disorder (ADHD). Most of the medicines used to treat this disorder last twelve hours or less. So, a youth may take medication at 7:00 a.m. to help organize the school setting and homework, but the medication lasts for about twelve hours (some last less than twelve hours; very few last longer). The medication that helped the child stay attentive and less impulsive is now wearing off—right in the middle of your evening activity. The child may be hungry since these medications often turn off the signal to eat. The youth may begin to struggle to keep his words and hands to himself. While the child may have come into the activity with the "ready, aim, fire" approach to life, this child has now entered the "ready, fire, aim" approach. The ability to act with forethought may be limited, and they may struggle to pay attention to directions or teaching times.

Please note that ADHD is a biological condition. We would never think of saying to the child with diabetes, "If you work harder, you can make more insulin." Yet how often do we put together sticker charts and establish punishments for children who find themselves in the middle of a medication withdrawal that happens every day at that time. Parents often cannot give a second dose since most children on the medication don't sleep well.

One of the best ideas is to supply this vital information to the leaders. If the child is hungry, consider asking the parent to pack them a sandwich (or have someone on your team have one available) or arrange to have snack time earlier. If the youth needs to move, consider some of the tools listed under the sensory section in universal design. Provide options to the child or youth and information to the leaders, and you will have a much better evening activity time.

Some of our children and youth programs offer overnight opportunities—at a camp, retreat center, or a mission trip site. The responsive design plan set in place will likely need to be adjusted and personalized for this event. Provide your inclusion coordinator with dates and places as soon as you know them. Some activities may require thinking ahead. For example, you may be doing a treasure hunt in the community, but if one of your group members uses a wheelchair, what will need to be in place for that individual to participate in that activity? Thinking ahead is one of your best strategies and will usually provide great solutions.

Use existing people and plans. The church setting is typically limited in time and scope. Many children who will have a personalized plan often have plans set up by experts in a school or clinic as well. Tap into these plans whenever possible. Permission from the parent will be required. In addition, many churches have found key people, such as a teacher assistant, who are particularly gifted at interacting with and using the plan in place. Find out if you can observe that person in action, or perhaps you will want to hire that person to come for a few Sundays or evenings to your church setting, where they can model the plan. Doing so will not only create continuity for the child, but it will also allow your church volunteers to take comfort in knowing how to best interact with the child. Please don't ask parents to cover the cost for this person to come for a few weeks. Find money for it in your budget. Make church a place where the congregation covers the tab. If possible, make this true for any additional staff you might hire to help out on a mission trip as well. Please consider this a church expense if possible.

If you have a child or youth who uses specific equipment, consider purchasing the less expensive items to stock at church. For example, if you have a child who benefits from a weighted lap pad, consider purchasing one so the parents won't have to haul one more thing with them to your setting. If a child requires a specific spoon or fork that is adapted for their needs, see if you can afford to stock it at church. If you have a child with an emergency plan that requires certain items, consider stocking a backpack with these items so it can be easily passed off to the right people at church when needed. Having a written plan is critical to children with medical situations. Depending on the plan, you may be able to fill a backpack that goes with this child from place to place at church with the items required to carry out the medical plan, as directed by the parents.

If you have children who use alternative communication options, make sure the people who come alongside the child understand the system. Communication is not complete unless there is a speaker and one who understands what was spoken. The individual needs to know that people in the setting will understand what they want others to know. Also, if allowed by the individual and the parents, consider learning how to program the device so it can be used well in the church setting. By having answers to some questions or specific song selections programmed into the device, an individual can participate to a much greater degree. Programming in a knock-knock joke every week may also be a hit with the peers. Individuals who speak American Sign Language will also benefit from having a complete communication loop, for which you will need an interpreter. Bonus: peers may be excited to learn some of the signs as well.

Learn about any additional equipment that is important for the individual. If the wheelchair tips back to create more comfort for a child, learn about how it works to help relieve pain. If a brace goes on the leg for ten minutes and then needs to be removed and reapplied after ten minutes, learn how to do that. Make sure the team of volunteers knows how to step in and operate whatever items are part of the person's life—with the permission of the parents and with whatever training will be necessary.

Always ask the right question. We often focus on asking, "What *can't* that person do?" which only leads to very few strategies to try when writing your plan. Consider asking instead, "What *can* this person do?" If you know that this person can eye gaze at a picture to make a choice, then you have discovered a way for them to participate in the worship setting or educational setting. With movement, communication, understanding, and other areas of development, make sure you are asking the right question!

Take full advantage of the double-sided personalized plans. Remember, every good plan has two parts. There is immense joy in putting these ideas into action. Think about it, not only do you get to have Lilly learn about Jesus as part of the third-grade girls club, but the other girls get to learn from Lilly as well. The power of her presence in the group has transformed the environments where I get to watch inclusion and belonging in action. Your girls club will be *better* because Lilly is there. Lilly's peers will develop character traits you could never teach with some curriculum on a piece of paper. Lilly herself will be the instructor.

This book would have to be offered in multiple volumes if I were to highlight this item alone. The stories and examples of lives that have been altered and enhanced because of the opportunity to be in Lilly's group fill my days. Let me offer a few ideas and some examples.

The first book I wrote for congregations was called *Helping Kids Include Kids with Disabilities*. It was intended to provide a revolutionary approach to thinking about both sides of a responsive design plan. Peers need information. Sometimes it's general information about God and the unique knitting patterns that are produced. Sometimes it's specific, so that peers will be able to understand Noah and Down syndrome. Peers are terrific at being part of one community if they are equipped and taught to receive the gifts their friend with a disability brings to the group. The result, after watching such communities grow and blossom since 1989, is my unwavering conviction that God will use your efforts to change lives in powerful and significant ways for each member of the group. Make sure you think about what peers may need to know (with parent permission, of course). Make sure you use the gift of this person's presence to encourage understanding, friendships, and mutuality. Notice what is happening with interactions. Encourage the group as they figure out how to play and learn together. Together. Belonging. Teach it when they are young, and when they are old, they will not depart from it!

Consider carefully the age of the individual who has the personalized plan. Steer away from including that person with individuals who are at a similar cognitive age; move instead to creating community with peers at roughly the same chronological age. It is typically not helpful to have a twelve-year-old still playing with toys in the nursery unless that person can serve as a helper in that setting. Think of ways you can add items or volunteers to the twelve-year-old setting so that the individual can grow and learn in that place.

Sometimes parents don't want their child to have a spotlight shown on them or to be treated any differently in the church setting. Many churches have wanted to create a personalized plan, but the parents wanted no part of it. What parents sometimes don't understand is that their child is already being "spotlighted" in a negative way. Children without accurate information often create their own information and begin to pull away or ostracize a peer. Here is where the beauty of the universal design vision comes in. If you already have options built in, you may need to beef them up in that setting. If a group typically does not use a picture schedule and a timer but you believe this child would benefit from those items, consider introducing it as a tool for the entire group. You can introduce some strategies that aren't necessarily part of a personalized plan but are part of the universal design plan. Also, if peers need helpful information, consider using the puzzle piece lesson plan as a springboard for honoring God-given gifts and challenges in each person. Again, you are not singling out one person, but you are describing *every* member of the group. As parents begin to trust your support, perhaps they'll allow more specific items to be shared in the future. Remember, it's a journey that may have already included some hurtful experiences in other congregations.

Find ways to pass on information. Good written plans will allow you to add notes about good strategies that have worked in the past. Make sure you have a good handoff process between the children's leaders and youth leaders. Also keep in mind the handoff that will happen someday to the adult ministries. Keeping good written materials will give you a vehicle for passing on essential information when changes in leadership or ministries take place. Furthermore, consider inviting the leaders for the upcoming year to visit the setting in the current year. Watching a personalized plan in action is one of the most helpful ways of handing off and building the comfort level of the receiving team, knowing the ways the individual is already part of the community. They will see a vision for how to expand that sense of community into the upcoming program or grade.

Learning from Congregations

There are so many creative examples in congregations of personalized responsive design plans for children and youth. This book has already highlighted several examples from these age groups. For the sake of illustration, however, I would like to highlight the work of one congregation through the lens of the personalized planning process described in part 3 of this book and then provide an example of a congregation that offers many options.

1. Central Wesleyan Church, Holland, Michigan

The church board arranged several meetings with the entire leadership of this large church to have a training and conversation about the importance of including persons of all abilities. Responsive design plans were viewed as an important part of this initiative. They agreed that these steps would comprise the responsive design process:

Direct the process. For many years, the church has had an inclusion coordinator on staff who has done an amazing job of coordinating plans and interviewing parents. She has been a trusted ally for many families as she helps them navigate the journey both inside and outside the church setting.

Define the participants. The work of defining who participates is done by the leadership and with the coordinator's support. Sometimes parents will call to initiate plans because the church's supports are well-known. In addition, a general screening process is carried out at registration that will help facilitate conversations.

Discover the individual. The coordinator accomplishes this goal through interviews with parents as well as through observations and interviews with the child or youth.

Design the plan. Central Wesleyan has many options to choose from, and they are customized in response to the individual. Buddies are available to respond where needed; sometimes a leader within an age group steps in; and spaces are set up for breaks or for those children who are unable to participate for all or most of the time in the general setting. The coordinator works with the age levels to make every child feel welcome and experience belonging within the heart of their children's ministries.

Draw together resources. The inclusion coordinator has done an excellent job of educating the volunteers of the entire children's setting. She is spreading her work more generally over the youth area as well. She is respected, has specific training for volunteers assigned to her, but she knows the value of having every child and youth volunteer have basic information.

Distribute the plan (with permission). The church acknowledges that this has been a work in progress. There is a need to standardize how information is put down in writing and then passed on to the next age group. The coordinator's goal is to work with the staff to figure this out.

Debrief. Those individuals who have responsive design plans are monitored carefully, and the plan is subject to change as the child grows and matures.

2. Grace United Methodist Church, Naperville, Illinois

On their website, the church describes what they offer in their ministry of "opening doors for special-needs children, youth, and their families" and tells how to contact their inclusion coordinator, saying, "Our Open Doors Ministry . . . strives include those with special needs in the activities of the congregation so that all can appreciate their particular gifts and strengths. In so doing, we enrich the lives of everyone in the church and help to build up the body of Christ" (www.peopleofgrace.org/open-doors-ministry).

As part of the explanation of what they offer, notice how many parts of the responsive design plan are clearly present as you look it over.

The Open Doors Ministry offers a variety of services to families with special needs:

- Review of each child's unique special needs in confidential dialogue with the family
- Development of a resource plan for each child
- Training and ongoing dialogue with teachers and youth leaders in the implementation of the resource plan
- In some cases, one-on-one support by "buddies" of children and youth with special needs in church activities
- Resources on spiritual education and accommodations for families with special needs, available in the Grace United Methodist Church Library
- Educational seminars—open to the congregation and the general public—on the opportunities for service to families with special needs in the church

18
The 3-Part Plan in Worship Settings

Worship can happen in so many different settings and with such varied ages included in that time and space. This section will focus on ideas that you can customize to the places where your congregation engages in worship. It may be Sunday morning or Sabbath with all gathered, Sunday evening in an adult small group, Wednesday night with the youth group, Friday morning with the seniors group, or at home with your family for a personal time of interacting with God. Wherever worship happens, consider some of these ideas as you enter into the conversation with God in worship.

The Calvin Institute of Christian Worship released a document that contains ten core convictions related to worship. These are prefaced by the words, "Christian worship is immeasurably enriched by . . ." and goes on to say in core conviction number 8, "a warm, Christ- centered hospitality for all people. A central feature of worship is that it breaks down barriers to welcome all worshipers, including persons with disabilities, those from other cultures, both seekers and lifelong Christians, and others."[43]

To explain further, "These ten core convictions are not innovations. They are timeless truths from Scripture and the rich history of Christian worship. Today, each conviction remains theologically crucial, pastorally significant, and culturally threatened.

---

[43] "Ten Core Convictions," Calvin Institute of Christian Worship, last updated June 22, 2021, https://worship.calvin.edu/resources/resource-library/ten-core-convictions.

The importance of one or all of these convictions risks being obscured by cultural trends outside the church and disputes about the mechanics and style of worship within the church. This attempt to reiterate and reinforce the importance of these ten core convictions will lead, we pray, to more fruitful (if not necessarily easier) conversation about the meaning and practice of Christian worship."

These ongoing conversations are crucial. There is still much evidence that there is work to be done on core conviction number 8.

An article in *Relevant Magazine* on July 23, 2018, reflects on church attendance and children with disabilities.

Religious communities strive for their church to be known as a place where everyone is welcome, regardless of your background. But many U.S. churches are failing children with health conditions and learning disabilities like autism, ADD and ADHD. And this has been a persistent trend.

According to a recently published study from the National Survey of Children's Health, the odds of a child with autism never attending church were nearly twice as high compared to children with no health conditions. These odds were also significantly high for children with developmental delays and behavioral disorders.[44]

Research studies also point to a participation gap and church attendance with regard to adults who have designated areas of disability, such as the 2010 Survey of Americans with Disabilities mentioned by Dr. Steve Grcevich in a 2014 blog post.[45]

---

[44] "Report: U.S. Churches Aren't Inclusive for Children with Learning Disabilities," *Relevant*, July 23, 2018.
[45] Stephen Grcevich, "Adults with Disabilities and Church Attendance . . . What Does the Data Say?" blog post, August 4, 2013, https://church4everychild.org/2013/08/04/adults-with-disabilities-and-church-attendance-what-does-theh-data-say.

Both studies indicate that we must continue to have conversations and practices that support core conviction number 8. Consider the ideas that follow as a chance to strengthen that conviction and provide an increasingly accessible conversation with God in worship.

Puzzle Piece Perspective

Previous sections on infants/toddlers and children/youth offer valuable information that you can apply to worship settings as well but consider these unique statements as they relate to worship.

Examine your spoken and written words. As mentioned in the puzzle piece section, using person-first language (when you're holding a microphone or writing material for others to see) is an important way to communicate the puzzle piece perspective. Equip your worship leaders, announcement makers, pastors, and anyone who speaks as part of a worship service to use wording consistent with the puzzle piece view. "Megan gave birth to a baby with Down syndrome" will be much better than "Megan gave birth to a Downs." There are so many variations that honor God's design in that individual. Use the guides listed in the resource section of this chapter to gain helpful information on appropriate ways to speak that honor the God-designed image bearer who will bring gifts to your congregation.

Our written words are also important. Sometimes we use categories handed down from a tradition in our congregation and refer to a list in the bulletin of people who spend most of their time at home. We may say, "Pray for the invalids." I always shiver at that word as if anyone could be an *invalid* person! In many cases, a church bulletin lists the people in a congregation and the needs they may have. Carefully review this list to make sure you are using puzzle piece, person-first language.

Focus on the gifts of individuals. Worship is a wonderful time to focus on the green gifts in the individuals who have gathered. How can we discover the gifts and then combine them to help everyone grow in relationship with God and with one another? As we think of individuals who may have a known area of disability, don't let that cloud your vision of the greens that this person brings.

Sometimes communities assume that every person with a disability must be a good greeter and thus offer only one "job." This approach is profoundly limiting, and in many ways, it casts a shadow over God's creative and unique knitting pattern in each person.

Sometimes communities assume that persons with disabilities only have gifts to share one or two times a year at a "special" worship service. While some of these opportunities can be a fantastic way to share the puzzle piece perspective, I caution against limiting a person's gifts to that annual event alone. Let those who read or recite Scripture be used in rotation with all the others who read or recite Scripture. Let those who sing with joy to the Lord in a way consistent with the singers on the praise team or choir be part of that group. If you have a person gifted as an intercessor, use that gift in that way, along with the other intercessors. It's important to remember that there is no "Holy Spirit junior." If God has gifted someone to serve in a particular way, trust God to empower that individual in the heart of the community.

Sometimes you will need to consider creative ways to use areas of gifting as you work around and through areas of challenge or need. I have watched congregations provide "green time" in powerful ways:

- While it took purchasing a new monitor and spending some additional time transposing material, the worship leader was eager to include a guitar player who had a significant difference in the area of vision. He was part of the regular praise band rotation, thanks to some creative supplies and thinking.

- An adult diagnosed with ADHD was passionate about getting people excited about an event. Remembering all the details about when and where the announcement would be made as part of a worship service, however, wasn't his area of gifting. Another person in the congregation would never be motivated to speak in front of a group, but that person was very detail oriented. The congregation combined these two puzzle pieces, and one reminded the other of the time and day in email and text messages while the person gifted in creating excitement and energy made several announcements as part of worship in person or by means of video messages.
- Children in the congregation were afraid of the adult who was a wheelchair user. She had truly little movement in her arms and legs, but she totally enjoyed being with the children of the congregation. It was heartbreaking to see them avoid her and look at her with trepidation! The leadership decided to ask her to hold the children's bulletins on her lap so when the time came in the service when children would receive the bulletins, they went to her spot to pick up the special piece of paper. In no time at all, the children grew comfortable in her presence, and she played an important role in the worship experience.

This list could be much longer, but I give these few examples to get your own creative juices flowing. Also, I want to note that sometimes people are plugged into areas that are not gift areas, which can create problems or issues. One church uses an audition process for joining the choir. Those selected deliver music with excellence. When a member of the community who happens to have Down syndrome wanted to be part of the choir, this person joined without following the typical process. The result was a person plugged into an area that was not her gift area. It brought confusion and discord in a variety of ways. If the process for selection had been followed, that person could have auditioned and then may have been guided to enter into a true area of gifting.

Another congregation noted that an individual knew sign language and had a wonderful ability to make meaningful, worshipful motions. While she was not a regular member of the choir for every song, at certain times she joined the choir by signing along, not singing along. This was a gift area she could use in public worship. Be creative. Look for ways people can be plugged into gift areas that offer opportunities to serve God and one another.

Allow Scripture to speak. While there are many ways to choose Scripture passages for congregational sermons, consider choosing a text that will highlight the puzzle piece perspective to the whole community as part of a sermon. When leadership prioritizes and highlights the perspective, the community will follow.

Consider the seams between the individual pieces of the puzzle. Sometimes we focus so much on the individual pieces that we lose sight of the valuable teaching opportunities of the seam and how God can use the process of fitting us together. I was speaking to a group of pastors, and one pastor noted with great honesty that it would be easiest and best to focus on the ideas of universal design that really didn't "mess with" the congregation as a whole. Turning music levels up or down would certainly result in a large group of emails headed in his direction. To avoid that and the ruffling of people's feathers, he was opting to stick to the ideas that would benefit certain people but not upset the community. While I understood his predicament, a certain sadness settled into my heart on my way home.

As I think back to Zeeland Christian School and the puzzle piece community that has been in existence there since 1989, I see that one of the main ways God wanted to teach us and grow us as a school community was by means of the fitting together of the pieces. The growth that takes place in all the members of the community as the pieces are formed into one picture can create both tension and spiritual maturity. Sometimes people need to learn to "prefer" someone else. The puzzle piece seams remind me of Philippians 2:3–4, which calls us to imitate Christ: "Do nothing out of selfish ambition or vain conceit. Rather, in humility value others above yourselves, not looking to your own interests but each of you to the interests of the others."

Perhaps some of the beauty of puzzle piece living is found in the seams, where to make sure everyone belongs in the puzzle we practice valuing others above ourselves. The students at ZCS have learned many times over that we sometimes lay down our idea of the best recess ever to make sure a friend who is more limited physically comes inside with a giant smile from doing what that person enjoyed. Sometimes the study group does not get finished first because they are patiently waiting for the words and wisdom to come from a group member who takes longer to get those words from their brain to their lips. At the end of the experience, the eighth graders leave Zeeland Christian with an amazing ability to "value others above yourselves." They practice this every day, from preschool to eighth grade graduation.

When we have a chance in our congregations to practice having the music turned at a level that allows Bill to participate without pain, the chance to go without perfume or cologne so our group can be fragrance-free and Mary can attend without becoming nauseated, or the chance to listen to a message while Malcom listens with a piece of pipe cleaner in his hands so he can focus, we get the opportunity to practice living out Philippians 2! My heart was sad for this pastor and congregation who would miss out on an important way to learn and practice these words from Scripture.

Participation: Universal Design

Your universal design idea bank will grow as you embrace the idea of expecting persons with varied abilities to be part of your worshiping community. Allow me to get the brainstorming ball rolling by offering ideas in four categories: physical, technological, relational/training, and content.

Physical

It's vitally important to think about the space where you worship. Can everyone present use the bathroom and get a drink of water? Would *you* go somewhere if you couldn't do these things? Do you provide a suitable number of parking spots for persons who need accessible parking? Several denominations have created a document that allows you to go through your building, as well as to take inventory of the attitudes of those present, to give you an idea of what changes need to be considered in the area of universal design and your space. This is called an "accessibility audit." We have listed several options in the materials that support this section, although you may want to consult your own denomination or affiliation to see if a specific audit document has been developed for congregations in that community.

Provide spaces and give options that allow for movement. The time when people sit still and listen for extended periods of time is ending. Even those who study brain development suggest that the brains of younger individuals function differently from those of us who may be a bit older. In fact, a recent piece of technology will send a message to your wrist if you haven't clocked your 250 steps that hour. Sitting is one of the least preferred ways to spend time. While some people *must* have movement if they're going to be part of a worship environment, others will also benefit from that option.

Emily Vanden Heuvel, a chaplain for youth in a residential setting, provide some insightful reflections on arranging a safe and effective worship space for youth experiencing issues connected with mental illness: "Time is spent creating not only a safe physical space, but a safe emotional space. The worship center is open and warm, lights are dimmed, the rows of chairs are spaced to allow room to wiggle, and the volume of the music is moderate. The back of the worship center is open and free of chairs for residents who need to take a break."[46]

Some denominations and cultures already have a significant set of movements woven into the worship setting. I recently attended both a Catholic Mass and a worship serve at an African American Baptist church. Both worship settings offered ample options to move. While in one setting the movements were more scripted and expected of all participants, the other offered a steady stream of options to individual worshipers. Both settings, however, provide a welcoming setting for those who find movement helpful in maintaining attention or physical health.

For other worship settings, movement is not as common and may need to be added in differently. Also, those settings that "expect" movement as opposed to "offering movement options" may need to remember there are worshipers gathered who may find movement challenging. "Please rise in body or in spirit" is one way to give options within those settings.

Another option for movement within the worship service is to offer "hand tools" or fidgets to use within the worship service. Some people will bring their own because they know that having something to hold is helpful. One congregation decided to offer "pew pouches" containing items for worshipers to use. As you consider what might be in such a bag or bowl in the worship area, include items that are quiet. All Belong offers a fidget tool kit to get you started, but even gathering some pipe cleaners, pom-poms of assorted sizes and textures, or stress balls will be a great and quiet start.

---

[46] Emily Vanden Heuvel, "'Why, God?' A Trauma-Informed Worship Service," *Reformed Worship* 128 (June 2018): 22, www.reformedworship.org/article/june-2018/why-god.

You can provide other opportunities for movement as well. Invite people, for example, to stay seated for the message or stand along the sides of the sanctuary during the message. Remember, requiring everyone to "stand up and take a break" will potentially exclude those unable to stand. When you give options, however, you're giving people the freedom to make individual choices.

You may have an area in the back of the worship center where you can offer alternative seating options for those gathered. Perhaps you have some soft seat cushions for those unable to tolerate the hard pews or benches. Add to your collection some wiggle seats so that people who choose to can sit on a cushion of air. Wiggle cushions or wobble stools can make a terrific addition to items that people can grab as they head into the worship center. Remember to include a note on your website or in your weekly bulletin so people know these items are available.

If you are creating the message for the week, consider planting a movement or gesture during the time of spoken word. Invite people to join you in making that movement if they wish. If you are leading in song, are there ways to welcome clapping, swaying, or dancing during that time? Can people join in prayer using different postures expressed in Scripture—standing, kneeling, lying on the ground, sitting. By "welcoming biblical forms" of singing and praying, you are opening the doors to movement. Again, these options will need to be filtered through your own traditions but consider how you can give options for movement in ways you haven't yet considered.

Some communities schedule in a "life together" or "greeting time" as part of worship. It allows people enough time to stand, get a cup of coffee, or use the restroom at a certain point in the service. This practice may be a welcome addition in your congregation as well.

As you introduce some of these items or practices, don't forget to inform your congregation. They will need to understand why some changes are taking place. You may say or print something like this: "As we begin worship today, I want you to notice that we have some new items and options available. As the psalmist says in Psalm 139, God "knit us together" before we were even born. The pattern for that knitting job in each of us is amazing and diverse. Some find it easy to sit and focus for an hour. Others find it easier to participate with movement options. In honor of God's creative design, we want to provide options for each of God's children as we interact in worship. Feel free to use the tools and invitations to movement as we honor our Creator God and worship together today."

Though we covered the concept of sensory differences in the children and youth section of this book, the insights bear repeating in the worship section as well. Sensory processing is a fascinating topic in a worship setting, given the many individual preferences as well as the extreme distress it can cause some individuals. If you are on the autism spectrum, you will have one or more sensory areas that are wired differently. Many people with ADHD, learning differences, or physical differences experience this as well. Some people just have a sensory processing disorder. It can last for a season of time or for a lifetime.

As you may have guessed, we have far more than five sensory systems; any one of which may be wired in a way that is either undersensitive or oversensitive to input. It may impact one sensory system or multiple systems. Occupational therapists have done extensive study of these issues and know how to give great support to individuals who may have these differences.

Be aware that many people experience these differences most acutely when the body is growing and changing. Sometimes middle school and high school leaders will see a huge resurgence of the sensory difference when puberty hits and the body is flooded with hormones and growth. Preschool and kindergarten leaders will see this as well. Given the changes to the brain, it's also common to see upticks in sensory difference in those who are aging. Persons with dementia, for example, can have great sensitivity to sounds and movement.

Here's the good news. We have many tools and strategies that can help. As we gather and expect persons of varied abilities to be together, you *will* have people present who have significant sensory differences.

In his book *Mental Health and the Church*, Dr. Stephen Grcevich notes, "The most significant strategy for including persons with sensory processing differences involves a thorough review of your key facilities and ministry environments to identify sources of excessive sensory stimulation that can be remedied at a modest cost and minimal disruption to worship experiences and church traditions."[47] He goes on to mention issues related to lighting, flooring, window treatments, wall color, fragrance-free zones, sound, and seating.

In many ways, we can learn from the industry around us. Movie theaters are now creating "sensory-friendly showings," which means they keep the sound down, lights up, and allow for movement within that setting. In the past few years, I've noticed that many churches have followed suit. They have thought through their spaces, and often through the use of Livestream, they have created a second space inside the church where families and individuals can worship. It's generally a smaller setting where the sound can be regulated to a lower level, lights adapted to be calming, and movement and varied seating options encouraged.

Other congregations are converting a space into a "sensory room." While this type of room can take many forms, the space provides an

---

[47] Stephen Grcevich, *Mental Health and the Church* (Grand Rapids: Zondervan, 2018), 154.

option for individuals who may find the greater worship setting overwhelming. Many times, these resemble the second worship space but may include specialized equipment and activities so that people can take a break in this calming area.

I have referenced a few of these ideas in other sections, but imagine how in this setting we can learn to prefer one another with the following:

- Regulating sound levels so they fall within an acceptable range.
- Offering a fragrance-free area in your worship space and the common spaces. Take time to examine the scents of the cleaning products you use and the soap dispensers in bathroom areas. Also consider the effects of using scented candles or incense in worship.
- Thinking through sound, movement, and fragrance issues in both children and youth worship spaces and adult spaces. While many people tend to believe that all children and youth love strobe lights and loud noises, this couldn't be further from the truth.
- Equipping your decorating team with the book by Dr. Stephen Grcevich so they can think about the colors, patterns, window treatments, and lighting when setting up a worship area.
- Connecting with a local organization or occupational therapist to give advice on that sensory-friendly worship space or room.

Technological

We have an amazing number of items at our fingertips that simply did not exist many years ago. My own children find it hard to believe my accounts of my childhood home with no microwave oven, no computer, no digital clocks, and a telephone where you actually stuck your finger into a circular plate with round holes and turned it seven to ten times to call someone's home. Plus, we didn't have contact lists inside our phones; we had to look up phone numbers in in something called a phone book.

My home looks quite different now. I have "embraced technology" with my smartphone on my hip, streaming options on my TV, and an internet that works at a fast clip to keep all our systems up and running. While the Newman home may be considered as filled with "modern conveniences," many persons with disabilities depend on technological advances to interact with life each day. Reading, writing, and speaking sometimes hinges on the right device or on internet access. Since we are expecting persons of varied abilities to be part of worship, perhaps we should think through the gifts that technology can bring to that setting as well.

As mentioned in other segments of this book, start by offering on your website a "hotel-type preview" of the worship setting. When I visit churches, I always see if there is some kind of welcome preview on the website. It allows me to choose clothing. It allows me to know if I would be able to raise my hands during praise and worship time or if that isn't a custom in the congregation. I may be able to recognize the face of the pastor, or some key leaders introduced during that preview. If the preview shows even one person with a visible disability, the church has communicated volumes in that preview. Consider making a "hotel-type" worship welcome and watch people enter more freely. Some will require this to attend, and others will simply enjoy it. If you do not yet have a website, consider putting together a "Welcome to Worship at _____" booklet and make it available to those who want a copy.

Advertise what you already have in place for persons with varied abilities and what you would be willing to arrange with advance notice. It's surprising to me how many congregations have hearing loops, large-print hymnals, and a gluten-free option for the Lord's Supper, but they don't let people know. Good ideas hidden away make no sense at all. Consider putting these notices on your website and post them in key locations in the church itself. Also consider advertising that you invite requests for accommodations and share the process for making that request. For example, if a person were to request a sign language interpreter, could you honor that request if it is made one week in advance? What if a person with a significant peanut allergy is going to be attending your midweek potluck? With advance notice, will you be able to welcome that individual?

Make written materials available ahead of time as well. From the order of worship to the sermon notes to the bulletin or newsletter, some individuals can better interact with the materials if downloaded to a personal device. A person who is unable to see the projection screen may be able to change the contrast or size on a personal device that allows participation in new ways. An individual may have a printer at home that can produce the document in braille and make that portion of worship accessible. Giving people access in advance to the order of worship may help a person who tends to feel anxious about a larger setting know that there is a beginning and end to the experience and thus feel okay about coming. Schedules for some people are helpful; for others they will be the deciding factor in whether to attend or not attend.

Use technology to create options in the worship service. An individual who may not speak a prayer request into a microphone in front of others may appreciate the option to text a request to a specific phone number during that time. Another person may prefer to enter visitor or attendance information on a website as opposed to handwriting the information on a welcome pad that is passed down the pew. People may want to read the pew Bible, or you could offer the invitation to read along on a personal device. As you think about your order of worship, ask if there are options or alternate ways people can enter into each part of the worship service.

There are times when people will join in worship if a live video feed option is offered. Live video is a gift to many individuals and families to help them stay connected during times when attending the service in person is simply not an option. If you offer this option, remember to acknowledge those attending via live video by mentioning in your welcome: "Welcome to Faith Church, those who are joining us here in the sanctuary and those joining us via live video." It lets people know they are part of the worshiping community. Are there ways that those joining via video can participate in tithing or in sending a prayer request? Consider ways to include the video participants as part of what you do each week. Livestream and Facebook Live are two options for doing this, but there are many ways to go about it.

Use your technology system to capture and display main points, key directions, or illustrations. When people hear the words and pair them with the visuals, it can be immensely helpful. For example, I've been in many churches where the pastor tries to verbally explain how and when to partake of the Lord's Supper. Sometimes lanes are identified for walking forward and others for going back to a seat. Sometimes people are to wait and partake together and sometimes not. It can be very confusing when instructions are only given verbally. A simple picture or printed bullet points giving instructions will help some people better understand the process. This can also be true of key points in a sermon or message. By highlighting the main points of the sermon with written words and/or pictures, some will be better able to take in the message. Consider how to work closely with those on your technology team to help make this happen.

Speaking of the technology team, make sure you are aware of the print size and display recommendations for projection so your words will be able to be seen by the greatest number of participants. Jamming sixty-seven words up on a PowerPoint slide in purple on lilac background will not be the most helpful.

Finally, turn it down! In some cases, turn it up! Again, there are guidelines for a safe level of volume for those gathered. As you regulate the sound, remember that some will enjoy loud volume while others will head for the door if it's too loud. We just addressed sensory differences and worship in the previous section on physical considerations, but please note the resource on safe levels of sound for those in attendance. By using standards set by an outside group with expertise in this area, you will have an excellent response if people talk with you about the sound levels you use in church gatherings.

As technology continues to change our world, the ideas in this book will undoubtedly become dated. Use your knowledge of what is available to you through technology and find ways to use this tool to enhance and broaden the worship experience for those gathered.

Relational/Training

The opportunity to gather together as one body in Christ allows for growth and understanding. Sometimes, however, it's important to *equip* all those who are gathered to best interact with one another.

Here are some ideas to get you thinking about what the entire community may need to best worship together.

Start by preparing the congregation to receive the gifts that each one brings. Everyone brings a perspective and attitude toward persons with disabilities. It may come from experience or from a movie or television show. It will often come from a lack of opportunity to learn with and from a person with a disability. For this reason, some members of your congregation will be unaware that persons with disabilities bring gifts to share with others in the body of Christ. Continue to bring the puzzle piece perspective to the entire community so there can be an expectation of giving and receiving from each person present in worship.

Provide information and training. Over the course of many years of supporting environments that include persons of varied abilities, providing accurate, honest, and Scripture-based information has come up as one of the most crucial factors in creating communities of belonging. People will form some type of reaction to what they see, hear, or experience. By coming alongside people with information that can help interpret what they see, hear, or experience, you have increased the opportunity for understanding and relationship.

We often talk about handing out pairs of eyeglasses through which others can view the person with a disability. It allows you to make sense of what you see and gives you a chance to interpret the situation correctly. For example, I know there are times when someone calls my name or greets me, and I don't respond. Some of you may interpret that as, *Well, that woman is so arrogant. She marches around the building and won't even acknowledge us.* Another one thinks, *I suppose I am unworthy of her attention. I feel terrible about bothering her in the first place.* Both of those interpretations would make me feel awful. The truth is, I have a moderate hearing loss in my left ear. I wear a hearing aid, but it doesn't work well in all settings—especially with noisy background sounds. I would much rather that people know about my hearing loss than to imagine some other false reason why I did not respond to their greeting.

Providing information to leaders, congregation members, and to those in children and youth settings will be critical as you embrace the idea of expecting persons with varied abilities to be part of worship. Here are a few ideas to get you started.

- Offer adult education opportunities to learn more about areas of disability.
- Stock your library or staff resource shelf with key books or trainings on the topic.
- Offer a training to your greeters, ushers, and those who may be the first point of contact for those visiting and attending.

- Use typical training and equipping times to offer information related to building communities of belonging. For example, as your youth volunteers come together in September, as your governing board has a retreat, as your worship committee forms for the year, make sure one of your agenda items is devoted to giving information about how to best prepare as you expect persons of all abilities to be part of that setting.
- Look at ways to add words and pictures to your website and weekly bulletin or newsletters that portray a community of people of all abilities. Do the pictures on your website show anyone with a visible area of disability? Do you have a welcome statement that indicates you are accessible? These words and pictures that are seen by all communicate so much to all who are gathered. In many ways, these are powerful training tools.
- Do you have a member of your leadership team or a person in your congregation with a disability who would be willing to tell a story or provide some information? While it's great to have training tools available, learning directly from a person with a disability who is already part of the community is the best. What does this person appreciate about your congregation and the worship experience? What is difficult? Giving that information to the worship planning team, the children's ministry director, or the congregation as a whole can help give guidance in this area.
- Move away from one special service each year that highlights "disability awareness" and move toward weekly or monthly opportunities to celebrate "belonging" or "inclusion awareness." By planting a key sermon illustration, choosing to highlight a particular passage of Scripture, using the gifts of a person with a disability to read Scripture or pray, highlighting a story in your bulletin or newsletter that celebrates an aspect of friendship and belonging, or "noticing" the green gift areas in members of your congregation that you celebrate as a community, you make the idea of living as one body together

in Christ something that is foundational for your congregation. It's not something that's part of a "special" week, "special" day, or "special" treasure. It's just normal for your community.

In addition to the "hotel-type preview" of worship mentioned in the technology section, there are other ways to allow people to experience a worship setting, or pieces of a worship setting, before it happens. How can you invite people to learn how to do worship before you gather?

I was visiting a church, and in the announcements the pastor mentioned the Baptism Sunday scheduled to take place next week. If you were a follower of Jesus and had never been baptized, this was your chance. You could sign up at the welcome station. It dawned on me how many followers of Jesus have not chosen to be baptized because they had been given no information about how it works and what to expect. After doing some investigation, they may have had a better response to the sign-up if the pastor had said, "If you want to learn more about what baptism involves, you can go to that section on our website, pick up an 'FAQ 'sheet from the information station, or ask that a pastor contact you this week with specifics." We often assume that people will know the rules and procedures for so much of what we offer.

Some people would appreciate an opportunity to come into your worship area when it is empty. Offering a 1:00–2:00 p.m. Saturday "worship open house" from time to time when someone is setting up the worship area would allow a guest to look around, get comfortable in that setting without being surrounding by a crowd of people, and ask questions of the person setting up. The visitor may also be given a "reserved" sign to put on a seat, so they know exactly where to sit the next day during the 10:00 a.m. worship time.

In addition, there may be groups of people who are now going to be part of a worship setting that is new for them. For example, children going from grade 2 to grade 3 may have a surprise in store for them, since the children's offering is no longer available to them during the worship service. They will now be participants along with everyone older than they are. Take time to transition this group of children. Bring them into the worship area when it's empty and allow them to explore. Ask the pastor or a key worship leader to talk to them about how they can be part of the worship time. Teach and practice certain things you will ask them to do so that they are ready—for example, to know how to pass the peace and what to say. Separate out the pieces of a worship service and give them guidance on how to be part of those times.

Make a booklet that people can take with them or download from your website with specific information about your time of worship. This could be written for children or adults, or for both. It would be something like reading a "pre-surgery" booklet that explains what will happen and why, which often helps to calm fears and apply a healthy dose of information to the situation. A worship booklet is a way to give more detailed information than what a video preview can often provide. Take advantage of this tool to cast the vision for why and how you worship together.

Content

As you plan your worship service, consider the following items, and get ready to add to the list as you think of ideas of your own.

Start by offering access to an order of worship. While many congregations have done away with the printed order of worship, some individuals really appreciate having a schedule to follow. Consider offering an order of worship routinely or printing a few copies as an option for people to use. You may want to have it available on your website for people to access or print. In fact, having an order of worship with both words and key icons or pictures will allow everyone a peek at the worship time together.

One congregation printed up an order of worship with both words and pictures and then put a check mark box in front of each item. The engagement of the children in their intergenerational setting was instantaneous. They were eager to follow along and check off items from the list. The organizer did mention that a child made a specific request: "We need way more check mark boxes in front of the word 'message.'" Next week there were five check mark boxes in front of that item. It worked very well in that community.

You'll also want to think about your spoken words. As mentioned previously, when you welcome people to worship, avoid the phrase "please stand and join in worship today." This beginning phrase will leave some people unable to join because standing is not an option. Consider this phrase instead: "Please rise in body or in spirit." Now you have allowed for each person present to choose to do this. You can substitute different words for "rise" and ask that people stand or kneel in body or in spirit. It's a stated option that may be a relief to those experiencing chronic pain or persons who use wheelchairs.

Build options into the Lord's Supper. Always offer a gluten-free choice as part of the elements. Gluten-free options have become easy to find in a world where many people have gluten allergies. The Catholic Church has a requirement to include some wheat, but the Celiac Society has approved some wafers that meet this requirement while still being considered "gluten-free."

As you think about partaking of the Lord's Supper, also consider the people who have difficulty grasping or passing smaller objects. Again, offering options can be immensely helpful. If your community typically passes trays down rows, you may choose to say, "If you prefer to be handed the elements or served by intinction, we invite you to the station at the side of church where this is available." Another option is to vary the sizes of bread cubes and mention that the cubes in the center section of the tray are reserved for those who need to grasp a larger bread cube. Whatever your tradition, consider a second option that can open the doors even wider for participation if people find it difficult to "walk forward" or "take a small cup of juice from the tray." Options open doors.

Don't forget, too, to think about those who may need instructions or practice on how to participate in the Lord's Supper. You may have visitors or individuals who are new to this practice. Think about your words and cues. Would it help to have printed instructions in addition to spoken words to give guidance on how to enter in? Look back at some of the ideas in the technology section about this topic as well.

Consider differing sensory systems. I invite you to revisit the section on physical issues and sensory differences as you plan worship together. Regulating sounds and smells in particular can make the difference between attending or not attending for some individuals.

Pair spoken words with visuals. Many of our worship services are primarily built around spoken words—an increasingly difficult reality for many individuals. If you think about the rest of our lives, there are very few other settings where people engage in a "words only" time for an extended period. Classroom teachers and public speakers know they have about four or five minutes of words-only content before they have to ask people to do something active with that information. They may talk to a friend about what was important, write down the best idea or take away from that time block, or think of a way to represent it in a picture, cartoon, or color. Whatever the strategy, if you want people to retain information, you must ask them to actively engage with the material throughout the presentation.

I have seen this done in many ways during church services. One pastor offered a way to take notes that had both words and small pictures on the note sheet and blanks to fill in throughout the message. An extra incentive was given to the children to bring the completed sheet to the front after the service for a piece of candy from his jar. Another pastor paused several times during the message, so people could speak to the person next to them and discuss for thirty seconds a key idea or main point. Another pastor had an artist up front with her. As she was giving the message, the artist created a drawing on a canvas to represent the words. Pairing words with these visual images was powerful. Another pastor used a simple "thumbs-up" and "thumbs-down" throughout the sermon to have people answer some yes-no questions or give input on a topic. For example, "How many of you have experienced something similar to what Paul did when . . ." This technique helps people be more actively engaged. Another pastor used a visual, picture-based presentation to accompany the words of the message.

Consider other opportunities to use both words and some type of visual to get your point across. One church wanted to invite people to a summer evening of fun. As the person giving the announcement was speaking, they had some pictures running on the screen to show people what to expect. Another congregation had a person "take notes" on the screen during congregational prayer so that the prayer needs mentioned during prayer were available in summary fashion in print. Another pastor quickly taught the sign for the words *Lord* and *hear* and then paused several times in the prayer to invite people to say or sign, "Lord, hear our prayer."

I could give many more examples, but hopefully these few got your creative juices flowing. You will want to think through the type of service you have and imagine ways you can pair words with pictures or other input to help people participate in a variety of ways.

Closely related to the last point, it's helpful to identify your "big idea" and "main point" of that time together. If you can articulate that idea, it often gives you avenues for tools and practices that involve a greater number of sensory systems.

Congregations have sometimes needed some convincing that it's okay to use multisensory tools in worship services. And while traditions and denominational practices will factor into the discussion, consider that God set an amazing example. "Do this in remembrance of" is used to introduce one of the most multisensory experiences in worship. Partaking of the Lord's Supper involves something we can see, touch, taste, smell, and often hear. It involves movement. I can hear God saying, "Do this and remember me, and I am going to make it totally possible for people I've created with varied abilities to be included through a multisensory experience!"

If you know your big idea or main point of the day, you'll be able to express it in words, in pictures, in an object for people to see or touch, or in an item for people to take home with them. If you know your main point, perhaps you'll have an item in a treasure chest that is revealed at some point in the worship time as "God's treasure for us today." It may be housed in a wrapped gift box so people can see "the gift from God to us today."

While sermons typically involve the greatest degree of creative thinking when a congregation wants to move beyond words alone, it's good to consider times of singing and prayer as well. Are there ways to add signs, gestures, streamers, flags, instruments, motions, dance, or different postures?

I have provided a large amount of information about the concept of vertical habits and multisensory options in a book titled *Accessible Gospel, Inclusive Worship*, but I want to mention that focusing on vertical habits is a terrific way to discover a common denominator language for worship times for all those gathered.

As a brief explanation, consider a typical preschool classroom where children learn not only play and academic skills but also when and how to communicate with one another. The preschool teacher is quick to prompt students, "Tell Mrs. Baker, 'Thank you for the snack.'" The students all respond with "Thank you, Mrs. Baker." Teachers coach students when and how to say, "I'm sorry" and "Please help," when applicable. But they're not teaching them the right words; they are also teaching them when those words are appropriate and how to think about how another person may be feeling. It's deeper than merely repeating words; it's forming language that will become a "habit" in the way we interact with one another.

The idea of *vertical* habits has a similar feel. We attend worship where we practice telling God, "I'm sorry" and "Thank you," along with many other interactions with God. While we may give these interactions more complex names in the order of worship (confession, praise and adoration, lament, prayer for illumination, and so forth), we can boil down these words into language understandable even to young children. In worship we learn the phrases and how to express those words and feelings. The Calvin Institute of Christian Worship developed and groomed this concept along with partners in several congregations and school communities, and they have several resources housed on their website. I had the joy of applying this concept as a tool to use as part of universal design for worship.

The initial intention of vertical habits was to make worship language less complex for new believers, but it is clear to many congregations how this is an accessible language for *all* who enter the conversation with God. Instead of calling it a "time of confession," imagine how participation can change when people of all ages and abilities are invited to tell God, "I'm sorry." This can be done with words, gestures, signs, or pictures. An order of worship can indicate this time in the worship service with both words and visual icons. As we found in the preschool example, this experience runs deeper than a mere repetition of words; we are forming a language that will become a "habit" in our interactions with God. This idea has profound implications:

> As I looked more deeply into the concept of Vertical Habits, it not only made sense in allowing a person with a disability to enter into worship and grow as a Christian, it also seemed to be a common denominator for all who are worshipers of Jesus Christ. Vertical Habits, therefore, opened the doors to inclusive worship opportunities—a place where all believers can practice these habits and words together.[48]

Personalization: Responsive Design

We've looked at responsive design in several settings within the church. This section will focus on some significant pieces applicable to a worship setting and then give some examples of congregations that practice personalization in their worship setting.

A personalized plan is birthed out of the desire for relationship. It's not just a program; it represents an opportunity to get to know an individual well and then imagine how worshiping together can happen in a more complete way. Though there are steps to follow in doing this well, remember that *forming relationship* is crucial.

One congregation had an adult member with cerebral palsy who lived in a neighboring group home. She had no biological family that supported her, and as the church worked through the responsive design steps that allowed her to be part of a worship setting, some deep relationships were formed. Because of this process, she ended up legally changing her last name and being adopted into a family from the church. The family did some construction projects to make their home accessible so she could be part of all the family gatherings.

---

[48] Barbara J. Newman, *Accessible Gospel, Inclusive Worship* (Wyoming, MI: CLC Network, 2015), 37.

Remember that members of congregations go through seasons of time. There may be people who will best be included in a worship setting through a personalized plan but whose needs change over time. A person may experience a stroke at the age of sixty-five and now can best be supported and included in a worship service through a responsive design plan. An individual may be diagnosed with dementia and benefit from a plan that focuses on ways to make the elements of a worship service more visual. There may be a child in an intergenerational worship service who benefits from a plan due to a significant seizure disorder and then finds growth and medical intervention altering the need for that type of plan. The coordinator can watch for these seasons of time and people who may benefit from a personalized plan.

The worship setting is one of the most important places to emphasize that every good plan has two parts. Too many times I've seen a great coordinator do all the right things in helping to establish a great plan for how that individual can enter into conversation with God in worship, but the plan didn't address equipping the worshiping congregation with the necessary information. Many pastors and worship leaders have received letters that say, "Joel was such a distraction!"—comments and emails that are often best translated into, "This plan does not have two parts." If someone is waving a streamer during worship to say, "I love you," to God, then others must be equipped to interpret that action. If a member of the congregation occasionally calls out during a quiet portion of worship, the community will need to understand the leader's perspective on that action and how it's part of the worship experience, not a distraction from it. That part of the two-part plan can sometimes be a longer process that involves equipping people in best understanding the individual, and sometimes it's a simple phrase the pastor inserts effortlessly as part of the gathering: "I'm starting a sermon series on

Jesus as our King, and I've asked Martin to wave a purple streamer today to help prepare our hearts for the message."

How can you distribute information to attendees so they can best understand and interpret what they see? This is what makes up the second part of the plan. If a person needs the Lord's Supper to be given in a certain way (perhaps by dunking the bread in the juice, making it very soggy, and putting it farther back on a person's tongue), then those serving will need to be equipped with that plan. Where does that individual's plan intersect with others? That's how you form the second part of the plan. Trust me, if you proactively think about this, it will save you from getting a lot of emails and comment cards.

Also remember that you need permission to share information publicly about a specific person, which can come from the individual, a parent, or a guardian. Don't forget, too, that any information you share with the congregation needs to be run through the puzzle piece perspective filter. Think about your words and the way you can describe the gifts this person brings to your community.

Honor the individual by making sure that the individual is involved in creating the plan to the greatest extent possible. While it's great to have a brainstorming committee come up with a speech communication device a person can use to read Scripture in front of the congregation, but make sure that person wants to use the device and is comfortable being in front of the congregation. Learn how a person communicates, and honor that individual by making sure this person is the key voice in the planning process.

A gold mine of ideas can be found in the book *Accessible Gospel, Inclusive Worship*. Each vertical habit has a list of ways to include an individual as part of that portion of the worship service. You can use it as a starting place and guide for the worship setting.[49]

Learning From Congregations

Congregations have produced many creative ideas to use in responsive design plans in the worship setting. Here are some pieces of these plans. Remember, the plans started with getting leadership on board, appointing a coordinator, identifying those who need a plan, and then really getting to know each individual's puzzle piece design. Here are some of the action steps that were part of the plans. To protect confidentiality, names are changed.

One congregation had an adult member who was extremely uncomfortable in social settings but still wanted to be included. The members noticed that one way she became more comfortable in other social settings was by using her phone to take pictures. This seemed to function as a shield from the hustle and bustle of the setting. They decided to ask her to be a worship photographer. They identified the area she could photograph and had her practice as the worship team occupied the stage area on a Thursday evening. They assigned her a seat and then also, with her permission, introduced her job to the congregation so they would understand the newly formed position of "worship stage photographer." While she only needed to do this for about a month before she felt comfortable worshiping without this task, the ability to learn about worship through the phone lens opened doors for her to that setting she enjoys to this day.

Another congregation had residents of a group home who would worship at their church. The six adults would come in the door, sit together in one area, and then leave right after the worship time. While the members of this group home were "in worship," no relationships were forming. With permission from the residents, they decided to

---

[49] Newman, *Accessible Gospel*, 33–80.

form an adult Sunday school group after worship and use materials designed to allow people of all abilities to learn together in this format (for example, Friendship Ministry's *Together* inclusive adult Bible studies: togethersmallgroups.org). Approximately thirty people came to this post-worship group and the residents of the group home were part of this number. The community formed relationships in this smaller setting, which quickly translated to new seating arrangements in worship. People sat with friends from this group, and the congregation no longer had a row assigned for residents from the group home. Now they truly experience worshiping together.

Closing: Two Experiences with a Reminder to Put God at the Center

Worship with Persons with Dementia

Together. That word describes many of the practices in this book; it is also the name of a curriculum produced by Friendship Ministries. It has been my joy to work on these materials that can be used in an adult small group setting that welcomes adults of all abilities! Someone called and asked if the materials would be effective with persons living with dementia. Great question! Given my close relationship with my father who was living in a memory care facility at the time, I asked for permission to try out the materials in that setting. God was about to change my world.

I organized two groups. One group had four to six members, including my father who was the one member of that setting with dementia. We met in the memory care facility and had a typical adult small group experience for eight weeks. After the first hour, I then led a group of fourteen to eighteen members who all had been diagnosed with dementia, along with three other members in our group to help facilitate materials and conversations.

While I came as a curriculum developer eager to field-test material, I soon turned into a learner. God grew me in ways I never expected. I can rave about the *Together* curriculum in both settings, but even more astounding, the worship and time together within both of those groups touched my life in powerful ways!

"Would you open with prayer?" I asked one of the members of the larger group who was speaking mostly in phrases and in words that often didn't make much sense. I watched the Holy Spirit invade his words as he spoke five complex sentences that could have been spoken as part of a Sunday morning worship service. Tailored to the setting, spoken with power, God resided in the middle of that prayer and in our group.

"Any song requests?" Once we met the request for singing "Jesus Loves Me," we typed other songs into the YouTube search line and found hymns that were clearly part of many, many years of worship. Breaking into harmony, singing every word— "My Jesus, I love thee, I know thou art mine;" "Jesus is all the world to me: my life, my joy, my all;" "It is well, it is well with my soul"—music and words filled the room. These were embedded deep into the hearts of the worshipers who gathered. Visuals, videos, Bible passages, prayer shawls, and so much more filled those two hours in each of these groups. We learned *together*.

I would leave each week having been filled by God and touched by Him through the members of the groups. In my one-on-one visits with my dad, it made me crave more time with him in sharing God's Word and recalling the great love of God in Christ for each of us. Our visits were transformed after this study. I came to expect God to use my dad's comments and expressions and moods to touch my life in some way. I listened for the ways God was speaking through him. I asked him to pray, and I prayed for him. As the words became fewer and fewer, we still shared a Bible verse or song together.

At one of the visits, about four months before Dad passed away, I held out my hands and asked if he wanted me to say a Bible verse (my left hand) or sing a song (my right hand). He looked at my left hand. Sitting directly across from him, I recited Romans 15:13 while looking into his eyes: "May the God of hope fill you with all joy and peace as you trust in him so that you may overflow with hope by the power of the Holy Spirit." He reached out to touch my left hand this time, and I recited the Bible verse again. He held up his hand and said, "Stop," when I got to the second part— "that you may overflow with hope." Then the words came out slowly as he pointed to himself. "Hope . . . for . . . me."

Tears came to my eyes, and it was clear that we were using the shared language of Scripture and worship to lead us to a discussion on what "hope" means for each of us in Christ. We talked about healing, heaven, and the hope we have in Jesus. As he continued to look expectantly in my eyes, I said, "Yes, Dad, hope for you and for me. Whether we are here on earth or in heaven, we can never be separated from the love of God in Jesus." He nodded. We connected. God was lifted up. And that hope is now a reality for my dear father.

I realized through my experience that God is not bound by the word *dementia* or *autism* or *bipolar disorder* or *stroke* or *learning disability* or any other diagnosis. His Spirit, His Word, is living and active. As we place those things in the middle of our times together, God instructs and blesses. It's true that the materials I used blend together the three parts our vision: *perspective* (each member of the group offers gifts, and we fit together like puzzle pieces in the body of Christ), *participation* (many options and materials that give people access points to the material), and *personalization* (knowing the individual and how best to engage each one), the most important ingredient in our time together was the way God invaded our time and honored the jigsaw puzzle put together in that place.

My Sunday Church Visit

Barry and I are newer attenders at a church close to where we live. As I left the worship service, I knew what I wanted to say to those reading this book as it ends.

This particular church is not necessarily known for any type of disability ministry. I'm not sure they've ever really thought about that concept in great detail. What I did notice is that the idea of a community in which everyone belongs happens somewhat naturally in this place.

My husband and I found an accessible parking spot close to the doors. We walked to the door, and I noticed one of my former students with autism waving at me through the window. He was rocking, smiling, and waving. While I heard from him the words "Hi, Mrs. Newman," I noticed he greeted others through the window in this way as well. I think he had appointed himself to this position, since his mom greeted me and wondered if I had seen him.

We entered a remarkably busy church environment, with chairs visible in a side area and a main worship setting with pews and a balcony. Clearly, we did not come in time to snag a pew, so we sat in the chairs off to one side. They began the time of worship (and yes, they would benefit from knowing about "Please stand in body or in spirit," as well as a few other tools), and then it was coffee break time. I noticed during worship that people moved freely about, and some even stood in an area with no chairs in front of the coffee pots.

People were welcome to greet others or enjoy a time of staying seated. Either was fine. Ann found me and introduced herself. "I'll remember you next week," she said. Ah, I could taste the statement of *belonging* in her sincere eye contact and warm words. Joy also found me. "I used to come here when I was living in the mission. We sat over here, but no one ever treated me any different. They treated me like everyone else. I also didn't need to wear special clothes, and they let you drink coffee during church. I'm still attending, and I love this place. I learned about who I really am as a child of Christ here. You will too." *Acceptance.*

They did have a great coffee time intermission before the message. Children left for their groups, people got coffee, and nearly everyone moved. A sign language interpreter was seated in front of a few people at the front of church. I wondered if the church set this up or if it just happened this way. No one paid much attention, and it was just a natural part of what happens in this church.

The slide presentation was clear and without background distraction, and it had good readability. Movement was welcome as part of worship many times throughout the seventy-five minutes together. The pastor had key passages up on the screen and was an engaging speaker. Several times he named what people might be going through—many of which were topics that connected with those with varied emotional states or physical concerns. It was all wrapped into an amazing message of hope.

One statement he made was this: "We are a ragtag, eclectic group of people." Pastor, I agree. In fact, I may have just fallen in love with this congregation because I clearly can belong to a group known as "a ragtag, eclectic group of people." This means you are expecting people of varied abilities each week—and each one can belong here.

The reason he cited was related to Ephesians 4:3–5: "Make every effort to keep the unity of the Spirit through the bond of peace. There is one body and one Spirit, just as you were called to one hope when you were called; one Lord, one faith, one baptism; one God and Father of all, who is over all and through all and in all."

The pastor noted that the Spirit brings this gift to a church community. With God's presence, we can have unity within this "ragtag, eclectic group of people." We can worship, learn, and live as one. *Together.*

While I invite you to "make every effort" to learn and add to the ideas in this book, mostly I would encourage you to invite God to come into the middle of your effort and direct each part. Be motivated to choose an idea to try because God highlights it to you. Be excited to enter into these ideas so you can taste what God is talking about in Ephesians. Be responsible and do your part, but know that this is God's church, God's idea, God's blueprint, and we are called to be faithful followers. Enjoy following God on this journey to "worship as one."

And now "may the God of hope fill you with all joy and peace as you trust in him, so that you may overflow with hope by the power of the Holy Spirit" (Romans 15:13). Hope for you and for me.

References

Anderson, Neil T. *The Bondage Breaker: Overcoming Negative Thoughts, Irrational Feelings, Habitual Sins*. Eugene, OR: Harvest House, 2019.

Calvin Institute of Christian Worship. "Ten Core Convictions." Calvin Institute of Christian Worship, June 19, 2018. Pages 35–43, https://worship.calvin.edu/resources/resource-library/ten-core-convictions.

Capossela, Cappy, and Sheila Warnock. *Share the Care: How to Organize a Group to Care for Someone Who Is Seriously Ill*. Revised and Updated. New York: Fireside, 2004.

Carter, Erik W. *Including People with Disabilities in Faith Communities: A Guide for Service Providers, Families, and Congregations*. Baltimore, MD: Paul H. Brookes, 2007.

Cornou, María. "María Eugenia Cornou on the Myth of Hispanic Culture." Calvin Institute of Christian Worship, November 3, 2015, https://worship.calvin.edu/resources/resource-library/maria-eugenia-cornou-on-the-myth-of-hispanic-culture. November 3, 2015.

———. "Universal Design for Worship: Consider Cultural Differences," Bothell, WA, October 24, 2018.

Fairway Christian Reformed Church. *FairwayCRC.org*. Accessed September 12, 2019. www.fairwaycrc.org/.

Grit, Betty. "Vertical Habits: Worship and Our Faith Vocabulary." Calvin Institute of Christian Worship, January 10, 2012, https://worship.calvin.edu/resources/resource-library/vertical-habits-worship-and-our-faith-vocabulary.

Grcevich, Stephen. "Adults with Disabilities and Church Attendance . . . What Does the Data Say?" blog post, August 4, 2013, https://church4everychild.org/2013/08/04/adults-with-disabilities-and-church-attendance-what-does-theh-data-say/.

Grcevich, Stephen. *Mental Health and the Church.* Grand Rapids: Zondervan, 2018.

Hardwick, Lamar. *Disability and the Church: A Vision for Diversity and Inclusion.* Downers Grove, IL: InterVarsity, 2021.

Hubach, Stephanie O. *Same Lake, Different Boat: Coming Alongside People Touched by Disability.* Revised and Updated. Phillipsburg, NJ: P&R, 2020.

Morstad, David. *Whole Community: Introducing Communities of Faith to People with Intellectual and Developmental Disabilities.* Bloomington, IN: Westbow, 2018.

Newman, Barbara J. *Accessible Gospel, Inclusive Worship.* Wyoming, MI: CLC Network, 2015.

———. *Autism and Your Church.* Revised Edition. Grand Rapids: Friendship Ministries, 2011.

———. *Body Building: Devotions to Celebrate Inclusive Community.* Wyoming, MI: CLC Network, 2011.

———. "Inclusion Tips for Your Church." All Belong, blog post, January 2016. Accessed May 29, 2022, https://allbelong.org/inclusion-tips-for-your-church.

Newman, Barbara J., and Kimberly Luurtsema. *G.L.U.E. Training Manual.* Wyoming, MI: CLC Network, 2009.

Open Doors Ministry. Grace United Methodist Church. Accessed May 29, 2022, www.peopleofgrace.org/christian-education.

Penny, Dr. Rev. LaTonya. "Universal Design for Worship: Introductory Reflections." Durham, NC, August 4, 2018.

Philo, Jolene. *A Different Dream for My Child: Meditations for Parents of Critically or Chronically Ill Children.* Grand Rapids: Discovery House, 2009.

Preheim-Bartel, Dean A., Aldred H. Neufeldt, Paul D. Leichty, and Christine J. Guth. *Supportive Care in the Congregation.* Goshen, IN: Mennonite Publishing, 2011.

Relevant. "Report: U.S. Churches Aren't Inclusive for Children with Learning Disabilities." *Relevant Magazine.* July 23, 2018, https://relevantmagazine.com/life5/report-us-churches-arent-inclusive-for-children-with-learning-disabilities.

Swinton, John. *Becoming Friends of Time: Disability, Timefullness, and Gentle Discipleship.* Waco, TX: Baylor University Press, 2016.

Tutterow, Mary. *The Heart of the Caregiver: From Overwhelmed to Overjoyed.* Birmingham, AL: Ascender, 2019.

Vanden Heuvel, Emily. "'Why, God?' A Trauma-Informed Worship Service," *Reformed Worship* 128 (June 2018): 22, www.reformedworship.org/article/june-2018/why-god.

College, Wheaton. "Stages of Attitudes." Wheaton College, https://www.wheaton.edu/wheaton-center-for-faith-and-disability/disability-foundations/stages-of-attitudes/. Accessed 4 Nov. 2022.

Wetherbee, Katie, and Jolene Philo. *Every Child Welcome: A Ministry Handbook for Including Kids with Special Needs.* Grand Rapids: Kregel Academic, 2015.

Winstrom, David. *I Choose Adam: Nothing Special Please.* Denver, CO: Lightning Tree Creative Media, 2017.

Witvliet, Charlotte vanOyen. "Speaking Well in Worship about Mental Illness," *Reformed Worship* 128 (June 2018): 12–20, www.reformedworship.org/article/june-2018/speaking-well-worship-about-mental-illnesses.

Yong, Amos. *Theology and Down Syndrome: Reimagining Disability in Late Modernity.* Waco, TX: Baylor University Press, 2007.

References, templates and more available on the website:

allbelong.org/worship-as-one.

Made in the USA
Columbia, SC
09 December 2022